DEBUNKING HOLOCAUST DENIAL THEORIES

*Two Non-Jews Affirm the
Historicity of the Nazi Genocide*

James&Lance
MORCAN

DEBUNKING HOLOCAUST DENIAL THEORIES

Published by:
Sterling Gate Books
78 Pacific View Rd,
Papamoa 3118,
Bay of Plenty,
New Zealand
sterlinggatebooks@gmail.com

National Library of New Zealand publication data:

Morcan, James 1978-
Morcan, Lance 1948-
Title: DEBUNKING HOLOCAUST DENIAL THEORIES: Two Non-Jews Affirm the Historicity of the Nazi Genocide
Edition: First ed.
Format: Paperback
Publisher: Sterling Gate Books
ISBN: 978-0-473-36228-7

Dedicated to all the white supremacists, neo-Nazis, religious zealots and other types of anti-Semites who either sent us hate mail or tried in vain to convert us to their warped beliefs about the Holocaust.

Without y'all approaching us this book would never have been written...

"You are entitled to your opinion. But you are not entitled to your own facts."

—Daniel Patrick Moynihan

CONTENTS

ACKNOWLEDGEMENTS

We wish to thank the following friends who enlightened us during the research for, and writing of, this title:

Peter Kubicek – For sharing vivid memories on life inside the concentration camps. For answering a million questions from a couple of 'goys' (or should that be 'goyim'?) and for doing so with humility that bellies your life experience and wisdom. For being a good 'mensch' and for teaching a little Yiddish and Hebrew in the process!

Marc Radomsky – For tirelessly documenting the Holocaust as a globe-trotting filmmaker and encouraging others to "claim the memory". For taking the time as an artistic collaborator to explain the current and historical reasons for anti-Semitism.

Pam Blevins – For reaching out and being supportive regarding an essay we wrote on this subject that eventually evolved into this book. For making a stand against those who seek to undermine history.

Nik Krasno – For providing insights from the Israeli and Eastern European perspectives.

Lisa Norris – For reading early drafts of this book and delivering intelligent feedback that forced us to rethink some things.

Gil Ben-Moshe – For sharing tales of anti-Semitism, both personal ones and worldwide incidents.

Professor Richard B. Spence – For explaining the various ways throughout history that paranoia has devolved into genocides and other crimes against humanity.

Zvi Spielmann – For inadvertently planting the seeds of activism against Holocaust deniers when our paths crossed one evening in Los Angeles many moons ago.

FOREWORD

BY HETTY E. VEROLME

This book has been written for those who believe the Holocaust is a fairy tale. It has been excellently researched by authors James & Lance Morcan, and they have proven beyond any doubt that the Holocaust did occur.

Those who deny the Holocaust are not only ill informed, but their resistance to accepting a well establish fact comes from a deep-seated hatred of the Jewish people. In other words they are anti-Semites.

Beyond a shadow of a doubt, the Nazis committed this heinous crime and the German people – who in the main were aware of the atrocities but kept quiet about them – are therefore guilty by association.

SIX MILLION Jewish people were murdered in a manner which can scarcely be imagined except in the evil minds of the Nazis who set about bringing to fruition 'The Final Solution' – which they very nearly achieved. In total, they murdered and slaughtered 11,000,000 innocent people without mercy, and this figure does not include deaths resulting from the battles of war.

As a Holocaust survivor I can speak of it as I did experience the terrible conditions for fifteen long months in Bergen-Belsen concentration camp. I vividly recall the hours standing for roll call during snowfalls, heavy rains, heatwaves and storms. We could not sit on the ground as we would lose our food rations for two days if we did.

They counted us, but the SS always concluded two or three were missing, even though this was never the case as there was no way anybody could ever escape the camp with the watch towers everywhere and the SS men constantly on patrol with their dogs. They often forced us to stand for three or four hours, and sometimes up to nine hours, during roll call. Young and old were meted out this mental and physical cruelty.

Food was 4 cm (1.5 inches) of black bread which was already weeks old. The SS had to put vinegar in the bread so that fungus would not grow in it. We also received three quarters of a litre of brown watery soup with a piece of carrot or parsnip floating in it. Those were our entire rations day in, day out for every 24 hours.

The beatings, the terrors, the unspeakable sufferings, the deprivation of water, the lack of protection from the harsh weather conditions, and being dressed in cotton grey and white (the colours of a slave labourer), all combined to strip us of our identities. We were only known by a number. *Number 10564 was mine.*

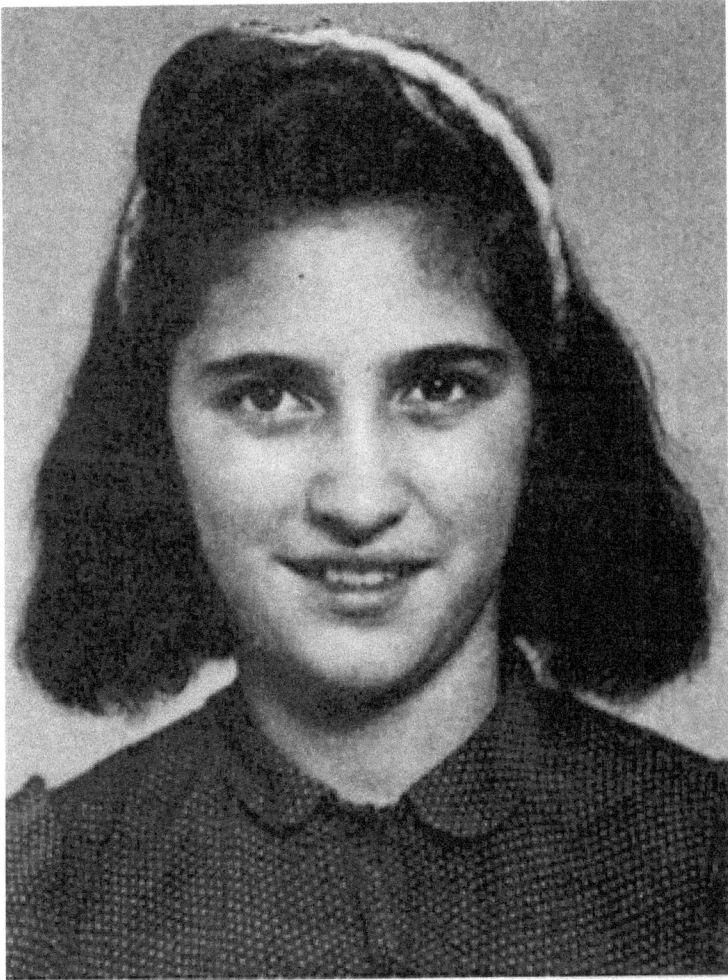

Hetty, zwölf Jahre alt, 1942.

Above: *Hetty E. Verolme-Werkendam during WW2.*
Photo courtesy of Hetty E. Verolme.

Above: *Hetty E.Verolme-Werkendam today.*
Photo courtesy of Hetty E. Verolme.

I was a 13-year-old girl when we were taken from our home in Amsterdam at 4.00am. Together with my parents and two little brothers we were deported to the transit camp Westerborg where we stayed for four months. During this time we saw many, many trains leave for Auschwitz. My father's parents were on one of these trains and they went straight to the gas chambers.

How unspeakably evil the Nazis were. They told the Dutch people that those detained would simply be put to work in Germany to support the war industry. The Nazis also told the Dutch public that detainees would be given a home and that the father in each detained family would work in a factory and the mother would stay home to care for her children. That's how the Nazis managed to orchestrate a quiet and orderly transportation of 105,000 people from the Netherlands.

On the 1st of February 1944 we were on the train to Bergen Belsen where for 10 months we were together with my parents. After eventually being separated from my parents it was my task to take care of my little brothers and also 40 other younger children. With the help of two Polish nurses we managed to stay alive as a group and were liberated by the English army on the 15th of April, 1945.

On the 1st of January 1945 there were 60,000 people in Belsen in an area not bigger than three football fields. By the 15th of April 1945, some 40,000 had died of malnutrition and typhus and in the months following the liberation another 17,000 died.

Of the 105,000 people deported from the Netherlands, only 5000 returned from the camps alive.

It is most important that the Holocaust is remembered. Let's hope this book will contribute toward that.

Hetty E. Verolme-Werkendam

Author of The Children's House of Belsen and Hetty: A True Story.

Foreword dated 3rd of June 2016

INTRODUCTION

This book is the result of the disturbing trend within some sectors of society to deny, diminish or otherwise undermine the historicity of the Holocaust – that cataclysmic event that saw the extermination of some six million Jews (as in the ethno-religious group of people) by the Nazis before and during World War Two.

Besides the obvious groups like white supremacists, neo-Nazis and elements of Islamic and Christian fundamentalist communities, there is perhaps one group in the 21st Century more responsible for perpetuating the myth that the Holocaust never happened or has been vastly exaggerated: conspiracy theorists.

We can speak with some authority regarding this as, besides being filmmakers and novelists, we have written a series of controversial non-fiction books that have led to us being loosely labeled conspiracy theorists. This despite the fact that in these non-fiction titles we mainly focus on factual topics or what we term "underground knowledge" – events, strategies, campaigns, deals and programs that have been overlooked or underreported by mainstream media.

As WikiLeaks' founder Julian Assange succinctly put it: "There are conspiracies everywhere. There are also crazed conspiracy theories. It's important not to confuse these two."

We generally research and write about topics supported by strong evidence substantiated in court cases, affidavits, declassified government files and the like rather than pure speculation. Important issues such as: banking fraud and high finance crimes, which decimate communities worldwide; media manipulation, which governments and corporations engage in shamelessly and which sometimes leads to unnecessary wars; medical corruption, Big Pharma, Third World poverty, the War on Drugs, the Military Industrial Complex...The list goes on.

Oftentimes, the abovementioned issues – and quite a few more besides – are conspiracy fact, or conspiracy reality, rather than theory. We believe it's crucial that people know about these issues and understand the difference between fact and theory in this context.

So, we hear you ask, *what does this have to do with denying, diminishing or otherwise undermining the historicity of the Holocaust?*

Well, as authors who focus on unearthing and promoting underground knowledge, we are sometimes approached by certain types of individuals who, collectively, form a dangerous element in society. Typically, these individuals may be conspiracy theorists; often they are amateur investigators and sometimes they're simply casual readers. The one thing they have in common is they are predisposed to regurgitating ideas they source online and debating historically-proven events – events like the Holocaust – as if they are up for debate at all.

Of course, the Internet is the perfect medium for bigots to capture naïve and impressionable minds. Often, those who buy in to the lies and misinformation these extremists spread are young, but not always.

We have written extensively about the Holocaust and its dark legacy. This no doubt explains why, in the last few years, we have received frequent emails from people – some of whom are even authors themselves – who question whether the Holocaust occurred as per the history books, and we quite often receive hate mail from anti-Semites.

If you are asking yourself whether Holocaust denial is really that big a problem outside of society's lunatic fringes, we would urge you to think about it in the wider context. While it is probably true the numbers of official neo-Nazis and vociferous deniers are not a direct threat to rational thinking or to the historicity of the Holocaust, many people – as in a big slice of the world's population so studies reveal – silently support such thinking and thereby buy in to this sinister underground brand of anti-Semitism. Such people usually keep their beliefs to themselves unless they are around like minds as they believe it's not "politically correct" to talk about the "true nature" of the Jews and their so-called *Holocaust industry*.

It's our assessment that support for these alternative versions of the Holocaust is far stronger than even the most frightening poll statistics show. For every one hard core neo-Nazi or outspoken anti-Semite, there are in our estimation at least 100 silent believers who have inadvertently been suckered into the twisted belief systems of the aforementioned.

Often these silent believers are confused young people who have a poor understanding of history and have been specifically targeted by those deniers who know the most gullible and easiest to brainwash are, as a general rule, society's youths.

This strategy of going after the young was revealed by the infamous denier Bradley R. Smith, founder of *the Committee for Open Debate on the Holocaust* (CODOH), in an oral presentation he gave in August, 1987 as reported by the Anti-Defamation League (ADL). In that presentation, Smith candidly stated: "I don't want to spend time with adults anymore, I want to go to students. They are superficial. They are empty vessels to be filled."

Denier Bradley R.
Smith

Public Domain
Wikimedia Commons

Smith, who referred to his tactics as the CODOH campus project, also said in a speech he made in Sacramento at an Institute for Historical Review conference in 2004, "I wanted to set forth three or four ideas that students might be interested in, that might cause them to think about things or to have questions about things. And I wanted to make it as simple as possible, and to set it up in a way that could not really be debated."

Surprisingly, or alarmingly, CODOH has not always been prevented from promoting its Holocaust denial myths in schools and university campuses around the United States. For example, in 2009, the *Harvard Crimson* school newspaper printed a paid advertisement by Smith which questioned whether the Holocaust even happened. This ad was universally criticized by students and teachers alike on the campus of Harvard University, and the *Harvard Crimson* hastily removed the ad with an apology in the next issue by the editor who claimed it was an honest mistake. However, there have been many similar examples printed in college newspapers around the United States including articles, advertisements and uncritical reviews of deniers' works in student-run publications at Rowan College of New Jersey, Northwestern University, Tulane University and University of Akron.

As of mid-2016, Amazon and other online booksellers offer numerous Holocaust denial titles, some of which are selling fairly well and appear to have a cult following at least. A few of the more popular Holocaust denial books include: *Did Six Million Really Die?*, *The Hoax of the Twentieth Century: The Case Against the Presumed Extermination of European Jewry*, *The Six Million: Fact or Fiction*, *The Myth of the Extermination of the Jews* and *Auschwitz: The First Gassing: Rumor and Reality*.

It's a fact many people worldwide don't believe the Holocaust ever happened. There is considerable documentation available to support this statement. For example, an exhaustive global poll conducted in 2014 by the ADL revealed that of those who have heard of the Holocaust, 32% (almost one third) believe it is a myth or has been greatly exaggerated.

More alarming still is that 26% of those surveyed harbored anti-Semitic attitudes. An interesting twist on this statistic is that 70% of those who harbored such attitudes "Have never actually met a Jewish person."

The ADL's poll – *ADL Global 100: A Survey of Attitudes Toward Jews in Over 100 Countries Around the World* – was no small survey. The countries surveyed included nine of the 10 most populous countries in the world.

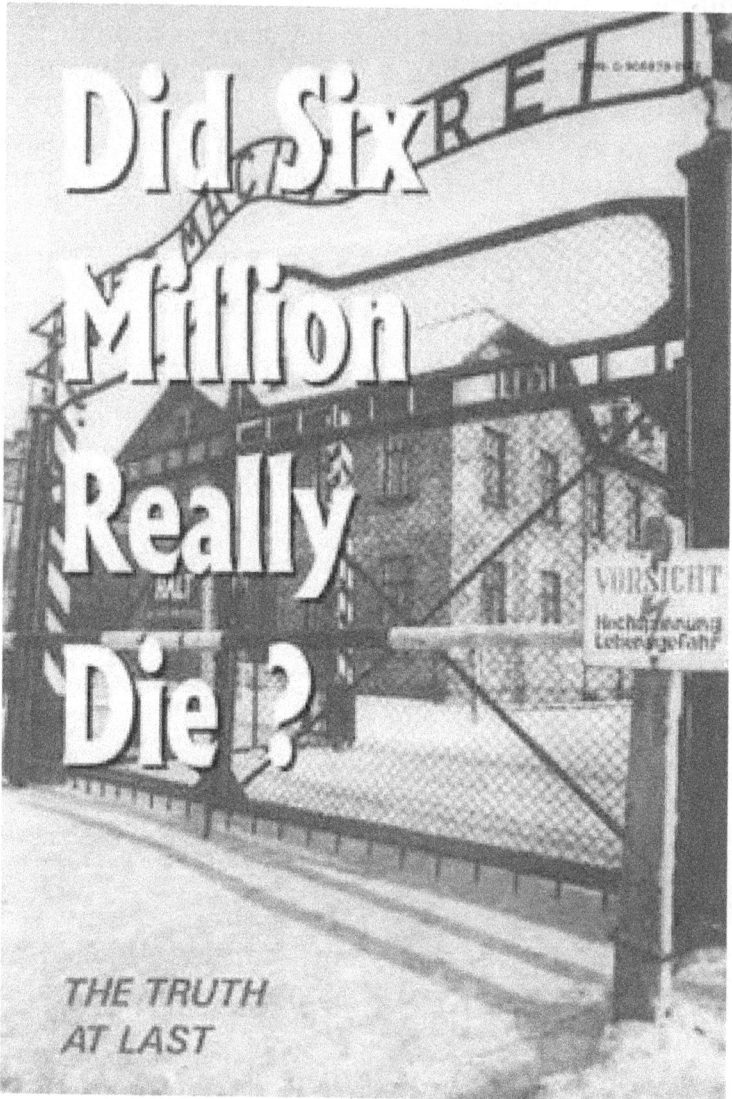

Above: Book Cover of Holocaust denial title.
Licensed under Public Domain via Wikimedia Commons

Another revelation was that only 54% of those polled had heard of the Holocaust. Referring to the ADL poll, Holocaust survivor Martin Greenfield wrote in a January 2015 article (as reported by *Fox News*) that "Knowledge of Auschwitz is likely even more limited, particularly among young people. Past surveys have shown that nearly half of Britons had never heard of Auschwitz. Some schoolchildren even thought Auschwitz was a type of beer." Greenfield summarized the issue well when he said, "For far too many, the Holocaust remains a mystery."

If you, dear reader, are unfamiliar with the Holocaust, read on – and be prepared to be shocked.

If, however, you subscribe to Holocaust denial theories or are in the process of being swayed by the denialists' arguments, we would implore you to carefully analyze your sources, check the credentials of those feeding you such extreme concepts and (most importantly) ask some key questions.

Key questions would include:

- Is it possible the authors of such 'information' have a subtle agenda?

- Do they speak of Jews as if they are inferior, lesser beings or even enemies?

- Do they try to shift blame for the Holocaust away from Hitler and the Nazis?

- Could it be the opinions you are digesting come from biased or hate-filled individuals?

Whatever the case, for those who believe in Holocaust denial theories, we challenge those beliefs, notions and concepts in the chapters ahead. All we ask is that you keep an open mind. After all, factual information can always withstand intense scrutiny and dissection whereas lies and falsehoods cannot. Right?

We believe the Holocaust is an extremely important historical event humanity must learn from if it is to survive let alone achieve world peace. It's not just a Jewish issue – it's a human one. If more recent genocides in Rwanda, Cambodia and the former Yugoslavia are any guide, the lessons of Nazi Germany have not yet been learnt. We suspect German philosopher of the late Enlightenment Friedrich Hegel was right when he said, "The only thing we learn from history is that we learn nothing from history."

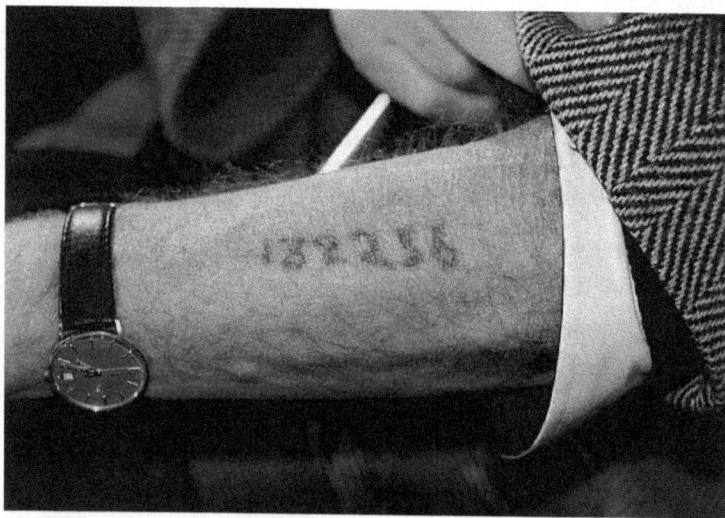

Above: *Nazi identification tattoo on a Holocaust survivor. By Frankie Fouganthin - Own work, CC BY-SA 3.0, Licensed under Public Domain via Wikimedia Commons*

All truth-seekers should study the genocide that was the Holocaust and ask themselves how on Earth this event was allowed to occur, keeping in mind *allowed* is the correct term as there was no shortage of witnesses, including those all over Europe who stood by and did nothing to intervene.

If those bystanders hadn't just stood by, perhaps the history books would tell a different story.

We have had the privilege of meeting Holocaust survivors. Seeing the Nazi identification numbers tattooed on their arms and listening to their personal accounts of the atrocities that occurred inside and outside the concentration camps during WW2, makes a powerful impact. It changes a person on the inside.

Unfortunately – and this is the key point – those last remaining Holocaust survivors are now in their twilight years, and as they fade away, the anti-Semites seem to be strengthening in their resolve to challenge the historicity of the Holocaust. Once the last survivors have passed on, the battle to preserve the truth will surely be more difficult.

With the publication of this book we, as non-Jews, are doing our small part to stand up for the truth. So let us state unequivocally here and now: the Holocaust happened EXACTLY as per the history books. Period. Fact. No debate whatsoever.

James Morcan & Lance Morcan

ONE

"The worst mistake I made was that stupid,
suburban prejudice of anti-Semitism."

—*Ezra Pound*

Here is a basic definition of the Holocaust which mainstream historians *universally* agree upon:

"The Holocaust (aka the Shoah) was a genocide in which Nazi Germany killed approximately six million Jews between 1933 and 1945."

The Shoah, incidentally, is from the Hebrew *HaShoah*, which appropriately translates as "the catastrophe."

Those who challenge the detailed and indisputable historicity of the Holocaust generally fall into two distinct camps: Holocaust deniers (those who say the entire crime of the Nazis never occurred and is all just a result of post-war propaganda) and the more common Holocaust revisionists (those who try to downgrade the death figures from six million Jews to a *mere* 50,000 or 500,000 maximum).

Note the revisionists are quick to imply that of the tens of thousands, or the hundreds of thousands, of Jews they acknowledge died, few if any of these "casualties of war" died in the Nazis' infamous gas chambers.

So, essentially revisionists are still denying the historicity of the Holocaust. Clearly, there is very little difference between saying *95% of the Holocaust never happened* and saying *it never happened at all*.

For this reason, we will only use the term *Holocaust deniers* from here on as we feel the term *Holocaust revisionists* gives them far too much respect and makes them sound intellectual or even academic.

"Negationism means the denial of historical crimes against humanity. It is not a reinterpretation of known facts, but the denial of known facts. The term negationism has gained currency as the name of a movement to deny a specific crime against humanity, the Nazi genocide on the Jews ... Negationism is mostly identified with the effort at re-writing history in such a way that the fact of the Holocaust is omitted."

–Koenraad Elst, Negationism in India: Concealing the Record of Islam, The Voice of India

We have studied all sides of this so-called debate. We've read Holocaust survivors' books and watched documentary footage of the actual Holocaust; we've listened to recordings of Hitler's speeches and those of other Nazis; we've watched footage of talks given by notorious Holocaust deniers including shamed historian David Irving; we've studied WW2 history and have met and interviewed Jewish survivors of the concentration camps. And we can assure you of one thing...

Holocaust deniers always have anti-Semitic beliefs and sympathies somewhere inside them. *Always.*

We need to point out not everyone would agree with that, however. The great American political activist and linguist Noam Chomsky once stated, "I see no antisemitic implications in denial of the existence of gas chambers, or even denial of the holocaust," as reported by William Rubinstein in the October 1981 edition of *Quadrant*. Chomsky later elaborated, in a personal letter to Lawrence K. Kolodney, by saying, "I was asked whether the fact that a person denies the existence of gas chambers does not prove that he is an anti-Semite. I wrote back what every sane person knows: no, of course it does not. A person might believe that Hitler exterminated 6 million Jews in some other way without being an anti-Semite. Since the point is trivial and disputed by no one, I do not know why we are discussing it. In that context, I made a further point: even denial of the Holocaust would not prove that a person is an anti-Semite. I presume that that point too is not subject to contention. Thus if a person ignorant of modern history were told of the Holocaust and refused to believe that humans are capable of such monstrous acts, we would not conclude that he is an anti-Semite."

We would respectfully disagree with Chomsky. Or at least conclude that he is perhaps correct *if* incidents of denialism are assessed formally in almost an academic fashion, but incorrect if denialism is considered in the wider sense, including what it takes to maintain such a belief system.

Above: *Anti-Semitic logo.*
By BlalckPestKommander - Own work, CC BY-SA 3.0,
Licensed under Public Domain via Wikimedia Commons

Yes, in the first instance someone could potentially be a Holocaust denier on the basis of reasons that are not anti-Semitic. For example, an engineer may have no hatred for Jewish people whatsoever and yet may dispute Holocaust reports simply because he or she believes it was not technically possible to kill millions of people in gas chambers over the course of WW2.

However – and this is where we would disagree with Chomsky – in the long-term, to hold to the belief that the historicity of the Holocaust is pure fabrication, or has been greatly exaggerated, requires that you also believe that virtually the entire worldwide Jewish community, including Holocaust survivors past and present, are liars and that they collectively make up what deniers callously refer to as the "Holocaust industry".

So, even if the original reason for an individual's denial of this historical event was not anti-Semitic, in the long-term it always leads down the "Holocaust industry" path the deniers allege is "slyly managed by Jews" who, they insist, are concealing the facts from the public.

In our opinion, psychiatrist Walter Reich, former director of the United States Holocaust Memorial Museum and now professor of international affairs at George Washington University, summarized the underlying reason for Holocaust denial best when he wrote in a July 1993 article in *The New York Times* that, for anti-Semites, "the Holocaust is an infuriatingly inconvenient fact of history. After all, the Holocaust has generally been recognized as one of the most terrible crimes that ever took place, and surely the very emblem of evil in the modern age. If that crime was a direct result of anti-Semitism taken to its logical end, then anti-Semitism itself, even when expressed in private conversation, is inevitably discredited among most people. What better way to rehabilitate anti-Semitism, make anti-Semitic arguments seem once again respectable in civilized discourse and even make it acceptable for governments to pursue anti-Semitic policies than by convincing the world that the great crime for which anti-Semitism was blamed simply never happened— indeed, that it was nothing more than a frame-up invented by the Jews, and propagated by them through their control of the media? What better way, in short, to make the world safe again for anti-Semitism than by denying the Holocaust?"

Deniers will pretend they are impartial and say they simply wish to report anomalies they've discovered in historical records, but deep down there abides a hatred of Jews. In some, or even many, cases their hatred may only be subconscious, as in partially hidden even from themselves, or it may be purely unconscious, as in automatic or reflexive, without them understanding why they are anti-Semitic. Either way, it amounts to hatred.

All too often, anti-Semitism is like a subtle form of brainwashing that is either conspiracy-based or religious-based. With the former, classic examples include the conspiracy theory which would have us believe the banking elite are all Jewish, or the age-old myth that the Jews control the entire world; with the latter, certain fundamentalists – most notably in extremist forms of Christianity or Islam – believe the Jews are an inferior people or practice an inferior religion.

"Thus, a story concocted by Mark strictly for evangelistic purposes to shift the blame for Jesus's death away from Rome is stretched with the passage of time to the point of absurdity, becoming in the process the basis for two thousand years of Christian anti-Semitism."

–Reza Aslan, Zealot: The Life and Times of Jesus of Nazareth

The David Irvings of this world are even more openly blatant about their anti-Semitic beliefs. After years of claiming he was an unbiased historian with no racial hatred whatsoever, Irving has since made disparaging remarks against Jews and various other non-white races. Just search online to find his interview with Australian journalist John Safran on the ABC TV show *John Safran's Race Relations* for an example of his (Irving's) vile racism.

In that filmed interview, Irving made such charming comments as "usually the (white) women who marry blacks are the ones who have been rejected by the whites" and "the gas chamber they show you in Auschwitz is as genuine as the fairy castle in Orlando, rather like Disneyland and Auschwitz has become the kingpin of the Holocaust industry" and "More women died on the back seat of Senator Kennedy's car at Chappaquiddick than ever died in a gas chamber in Auschwitz."

Irving also lost a libel case in the United Kingdom against author Deborah Lipstadt and her publisher, Penguin Books, which we refer to in greater detail in chapter 4. In the process, his Holocaust denial

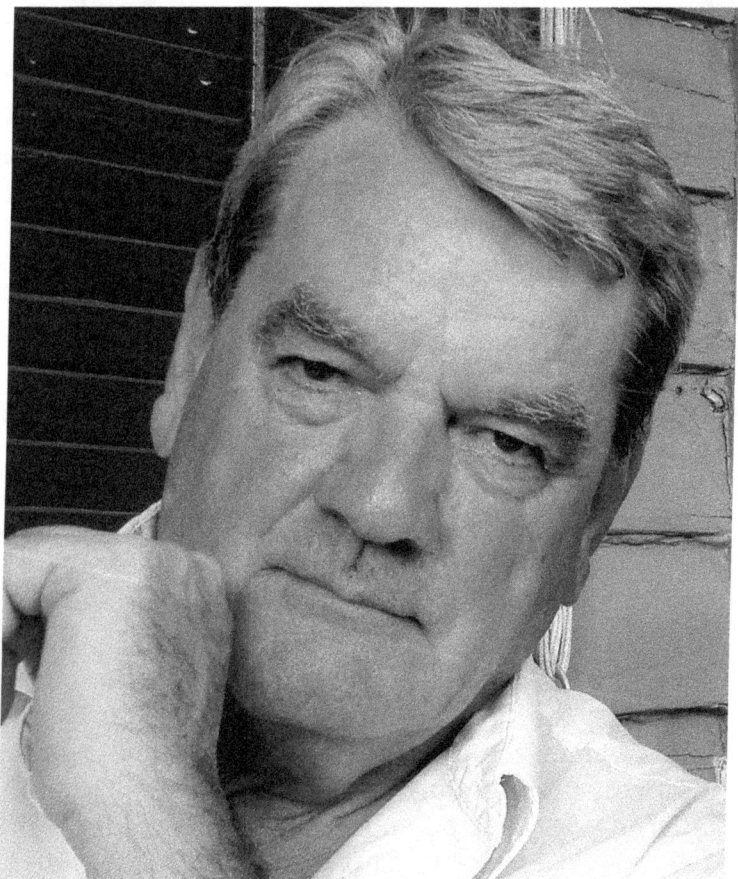

Above: *Notorious Holocaust denier David Irving.*
Licensed under Public Domain via Wikimedia Commons

arguments were historically and scientifically proven beyond doubt to be incorrect and a *purposeful* misrepresentation of the true facts of the Nazi genocide.

During that court case, the trial judge, Justice Charles Gray, concluded that: "Irving has, for his own ideological reasons, persistently and deliberately misrepresented and manipulated historical evidence; that, for the same reasons, he has portrayed Hitler in an unwarrantedly favorable light, principally in relation to his attitude towards, and responsibility for, the treatment of the Jews; that he is an active Holocaust denier; that he is anti-semitic and racist, and that he associates with right-wing extremists who promote neo-Nazism."

And there was the infamous poem written by Irving in an article headed *Irving taught his nine-month-old daughter racist ditty, libel trial told*, which was published in *The Guardian* newspaper on February 3, 2000.

That report states, "The QC read out a September 1994 extract from Mr Irving's personal diaries in which the historian referred to a poem he had sung to his daughter when 'half-breed children' were wheeled past."

An excerpt from the poem Irving wrote for his infant daughter follows:

"*I am a Baby Aryan,*

Not Jewish or Sectarian.

I have no plans to marry-an

Ape or Rastafarian."

So much for Mr. Irving being the 'unbiased' and 'impartial' historian Holocaust deniers claim he is!

An article on the United States Holocaust Memorial Museum (USHMM) website does an excellent job of summarizing the various ways people end up becoming deniers. Titled *Origins of Holocaust Denial*, the article states that many "deny the Holocaust for more overtly racist, political, or strategic reasons."

The USHMM article continues, "These deniers begin with the premise that the Holocaust did not happen. This premise suits their broader purposes. They deny the Holocaust as an article of faith and no amount of rational argumentation can dissuade them. This denial is irrational, largely unrelated either to the facts of the history or to the enormity of the event. Some people deny the Holocaust because of innate antisemitism, irrational hated of Jews.

"In fact, Holocaust denial has been called by some scholars the "new antisemitism" for it recycles many of the elements of pre-1945 antisemitism in a post-World War II context. Holocaust deniers argue that reports of the Holocaust are really part of a vast shadowy plot to make the white, western world feel guilty and to advance the interest of Jews.

"Holocaust denial, then, unites a broad range of radical right-wing hate groups in the United States and elsewhere, ranging from Ku Klux Klan segregationists to skinheads seeking to revive Nazism to radical Muslim activists seeking to destroy Israel".

The USHMM article concludes, "Holocaust deniers want to debate the very existence of the Holocaust as a historical event. They want above all to be seen as legitimate scholars arguing a historical point. They crave attention, a public platform to air what they refer to as 'the other side of the issue'. Because legitimate scholars do not doubt that the Holocaust happened, such assertions play no role in historical debates. Although deniers insist that the idea of the Holocaust as myth is a reasonable topic of debate, it is clear, in light of the overwhelming weight of evidence that the Holocaust happened, that the debate the deniers proffer is more about antisemitism and hate politics than it is about history."

Incidentally, the USHMM makes a perceptive point about Holocaust deniers. It reminds us the very views they perpetuate, accusing Jews of conspiracy and world domination, are the same "hateful charges that were instrumental in laying the groundwork for the Holocaust" in the first place.

Why should anyone be concerned by the existence of Holocaust denialism?

Well, any denial or distortion of a historically proven event is an attack on the truth. In the case of the Holocaust, persecution of Jews by the Nazis ended in genocide. However, the Jewish community weren't the only ones who suffered. Millions of other 'undesirables' died at the hands of the Nazis – a graphic reminder that when one race or group of people is targeted, everyone is vulnerable. To deny or undermine the historicity of the Holocaust at a time when anti-Semitism is once again on the rise worldwide, is to fan the flames of racism and hate; to tolerate it is to invite a repeat of history.

> **"Injustice anywhere is a threat to justice everywhere."**
>
> *–Martin Luther King, Jr.*

Above: *WW2 anti-Semitic poster, written in Polish. Translation: "JEWS-SUCKING LOUSE-TYPHUS".*

Credit: By German propaganda ministry, PROMI (de:Propagandaministerium) Archives of Institute of National Remembrance, Poland.

Tomasz Szarota (1973) Okupowanej Warszawy dzień powszedni, Warsaw: Czytelnik, pp. 48 no ISBN

Narodowe Archiwum Cyfrowe (Sygnatura: 2-11632) (Polish National Digital Archive),

Licensed under Public Domain via Wikimedia Commons

In the following chapters we debunk the most common myths Holocaust deniers perpetuate.

Some chapters, you will note, are written in a casually informal tone that borders on conversational at times. We make no apology for this. Some of the text has been lifted verbatim from replies we sent, mostly via email, to Holocaust deniers and other confused individuals who contacted us. We have retained that tone in places as we feel it best gets the message across in certain cases.

TWO

QUESTIONING THE CONFIRMED DEATH TOLL

"MYTH #1: "You could not kill 6,000,000 people in those facilities in Auschwitz and the other death camps! The six million figure would be almost impossible to achieve. It would have required one hell of a meat grinder, and a superhuman effort, to kill such an enormous number of people."

—Anonymous Holocaust denier #1

Actually, 11 million people were killed in the Holocaust – six million of whom were Jews. And note that three million Jews (50% of total Jewish fatalities) are estimated to have died in the Nazi extermination camps – victims of overwork, starvation, beatings, experimentation and, of course, the dreaded gas chambers.

This mistaken assumption that *all* Holocaust victims died in concentration camps, either by gassing or other means, is even perpetuated by supposedly intelligent people who have been "studying" the Holocaust for decades, or so they claim. People like

Mark Weber, one of the world's most recognizable Holocaust deniers. Weber, according to his mostly self-written bios online at least, has studied history at the University of Illinois, the University of Munich, Portland State University and Indiana University. It's not clear to us why he felt the need to study history at so many universities. Nor could we verify what degrees he has.

Weber, who is the founder of the classy-sounding but in reality Holocaust-denying Institute For Historical Review, repeatedly makes this very mistake (assuming all six million Jewish Holocaust victims were gassed to death) in an essay he wrote titled *Is the Holocaust a Hoax?* The article ran in its entirety on the *Bible Believers* website.

To state, as he does, "Though six million Jews supposedly died in the gas chambers" is Weber's first mistake, and it's a biggie. No legitimate historian has *ever* claimed, or even remotely implied, that six million Jews died in gas chambers.

And to state, "Even if we threw away all the evidence and accounted for every so-called gas chamber, it would have taken 68 YEARS to accomplish gassing six million Jews!" is Weber's second mistake as his genius-like mathematical estimates here are based on his first incorrect assumption.

Reporting on the rest of his clearly masterful and scholarly investigation, Weber goes on to conclude the Holocaust is definitely a hoax. He does so categorically and without providing any evidence – unless you accept *Corinthians 13:6* and other Biblical passages he quotes as evidence – and he states that "The time has come for Christian scholars and pastors to recognize this, and to stop perpetrating a hoax." He says a lot more besides, but we won't bore you with any more of his diatribe.

An almost verbatim mistake regarding six million gassings is made by another American Holocaust denier, Pastor Steven L Anderson, founder of the Faithful Word Baptist Church. In a video presentation he uploaded to YouTube titled *Did the Holocaust Really Happen?*, Pastor Anderson says "The issue is whether or not six million Jews died in gas chambers and were subsequently cremated."

No Pastor, that's not the issue at all. If you want to debate history with the big boys then perhaps you should spend a little less time preaching and go back to school.

> *"On one occasion, when he was about to be taken from the interrogation room, he thought he was going to be shot. His knees buckled and he cried out in a pleading voice: "I have not told you everything yet"."*
>
> –Deborah E. Lipstadt, The Eichmann Trial

Names like *Auschwitz, Dachau, Treblinka, Belsen* and *Sobibor* have a ghastly ring to them and will serve as a permanent reminder of Man's inhumanity to Man, but more about these sites later.

Besides the concentration camps, Nazi death squads and their European associates rounded up and massacred Jews in towns and cities Europe-wide. Referred to by historians as "open-air killings," around 1.5 million Jews are estimated to have been murdered in this fashion, with machine guns being the preferred instrument of death.

Just research the amount of open-air massacres in Nazi-occupied Lithuania (where 80% of the country's 220,000 Jews were exterminated in one year alone), Ukraine and Poland if you need confirmation. And keep in mind the wholesale slaughter wasn't limited to the aforementioned countries. Most of these massacres had numerous witnesses, are supported by photographic evidence and have been verified beyond any shadow of a doubt.

One of many such examples is Babi Yar, a ravine in Ukraine's capital city Kiev, where over just two September days (29th to 30th) in 1941, approximately 34,000 Jews were killed by death squads.

The *History.com* website details this event beneath the headline "Babi Yar massacre begins." An excerpt from the article follows:

"The German army took Kiev on September 19, and special SS squads prepared to carry out Nazi leader Adolf Hitler's orders to exterminate all Jews and Soviet officials found there. Beginning on September 29, more than 30,000 Jews were marched in small groups to the Babi Yar ravine to the north of the city, ordered to strip naked, and then machine-gunned into the ravine. The massacre ended on September 30, and the dead and wounded alike were covered over with dirt and rock.

"Between 1941 and 1943, thousands more Jews, Soviet officials, and Russian prisoners of war were executed at the Babi Yar ravine in a similar manner. As the German armies retreated from the USSR, the Nazis attempted to hide evidence of the massacres by exhuming the bodies and burning them in large pyres. Numerous eyewitnesses and other evidence, however, attest to the atrocities at Babi Yar, which became a symbol of Jewish suffering in the Holocaust."

Above: *A member of the Einsatzgruppen shooting naked Jews.*
Licensed under Public Domain via Wikimedia Commons

Above: *A Jewish woman in the Lviv Ghetto fleeing from armed Ukrainian nationalists.*

Credit: By Unknown - Lviv pogrom of 1941 in pictures (Axis History Forum) with external links and reprints.

Street identified Medova (Медовая улица).

Licensed under Public Domain via Wikimedia Commons

We have spoken to local Ukrainians of non-Jewish descent who confirm that in the western Ukraine entire towns that were almost exclusively Jewish before WW2 now have no Jews as all were executed by the Nazis.

Most tellingly, eyewitnesses to some of these massacres include high ranking German officers – one of those being convicted war criminal German SS-Gruppenführer Otto Ohlendorf, head of the intelligence and security division Inland-SD and commanding officer of Einsatzgruppe D task force, which perpetrated mass murder in Moldova, Ukraine and the Crimea.

In Herr Ohlendorf's own words, "The Einsatzgruppen had the mission to protect the rear of the troops by killing the Jews, Gypsies, Communist functionaries, active Communists, and all persons who would endanger the security."

The Einsatzgruppe's victims were in reality almost entirely Jewish civilians. And directly contradicting Ohlendorf's assertion that the mission was to "protect the rear of the troops," not a single Einsatzgruppe member was killed in action during these operations – essentially proof that the true mission was to slaughter innocent people.

In its first year alone (1941), the Einsatzgruppen killed 300,000 civilians, mainly by shootings at mass-killing sites outside major towns.

The United States Holocaust Memorial Museum (USHMM) has recorded the eyewitness account of one survivor of an Einsatzgruppen massacre in Piryatin, Ukraine, where on April 6, 1942, the Germans killed 1600 Jews. It reads as follows:

"I saw them do the killing. At 5:00 pm they gave the command, "Fill in the pits." Screams and groans were coming from the pits. Suddenly I saw my neighbor Ruderman rise from under the soil ... His eyes were bloody and he was screaming: "Finish me off!" ... A murdered woman lay at my feet. A boy of five years crawled out from under her body and began to scream desperately. "Mommy!" That was all I saw, since I fell unconscious."

Lawrence N. Powell, of Tulane University, summarizes the extent of Nazi open-air shootings on the Holocaust Survivors website *holocaustsurvivors.org*. Powell says, "The onset of the Nazi-Soviet war signaled the beginning of the 'Final Solution'. Most of the slaughter happened in the 'East'--in Poland, the Baltic states, the Balkans, and areas of Soviet territory conquered by the Nazis after the June 22, 1941 attack on Russia. Trial and error characterized the early phases of mass murder. Before utilizing gas, SS forces carried out open-air shootings, often with the assistance of local collaborators recruited from among the most anti-Semitic elements in the Baltic and Ukrainian populations."

Powell continues, "Following in the wake of German armies, mobile killing squads called Einsatzgruppen marched thousands of Jews into the woods and shot them en masse. Between July 4 and 20, for example, as many as 5,000 Jews from Vilna, Lithuania, the ancient center of Jewish piety and learning, were carried to fuel pits in the nearby Ponary forest, ordered to undress, and gunned down as they held hands ... All together 1.3 million Jews died in these outdoor massacres".

Beyond the concentration camps, and beyond the Nazi and Nazi-associated death squads, which

Above: *Einsatzgruppe members execute Jews in Lithuania, 1942.*

Credit: By Unknown

Licensed under Public Domain via Wikimedia Commons

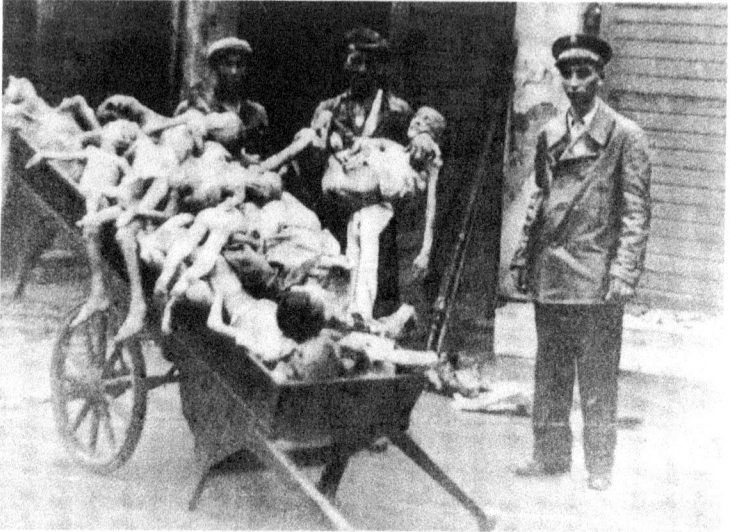

Above: *Emaciated corpses of children in Warsaw Ghetto.*

Credit: By Nieznany/unknown - Warszawskie getto 1943–1988.

W 45 rocznicę powstania, Wydawnictwo Interpress, Warszawa 1988, ISBN 83-223-2465-0
(photographs at the end of the book; pages not numbered),

Licensed under Public Domain via Wikimedia Commons

massacred large groups of Jews outside of those camps, the six million figure also includes about 500,000 Jews who were starved to death in ghettos in Germany and Poland during *and* prior to WW2. (Remember, the Holocaust started in 1933, so for European Jews the war began six years before the official commencement of hostilities).

Besides Jews, victims of the Holocaust included other races and groups deemed "inferior" by the Nazis. These included Roma Gypsies, Poles, homosexuals, Freemasons, Jehovah's Witnesses, Slovenes and disabled people. As mentioned already, persecution of these groups resulted in millions of additional deaths, contributing to the 11 million total historians arrived at.

Have you noticed how the Holocaust deniers only ever quibble over the number of Jewish deaths? Now why is that?

The answer is very simple: Because they are anti-Semitic.

It really is that simple. Anti-Semitism is one of the most aggressive forces on the planet, and has been since Biblical times.

Had the Holocaust been a purge of any other race or group of people, everyone would most likely accept the facts. Who, for example, disputes that at least 800,000 Rwandans died in the genocide that occurred during the Rwandan civil war? Or that around 1.7 million Cambodians died in the Cambodian killing fields?

Keep in mind the Nazis themselves were meticulous record-keepers, and they kept extensive documentation on deportations and deaths of Jews. There was a frantic rush, of course, to destroy those records in the final days of the Third Reich. However, many records still survived.

Human rights groups have recovered much of the Nazi and non-Nazi documentation relating to the Holocaust, and to date have found IDs for more than four million confirmed Jewish Holocaust victims who died (which we mention in greater detail later). Additionally, documentation relating to many of the five million non-Jews who died has also been recovered. This is all easily sourced in the public domain.

Make no mistake about it, most of the Jews living in Europe at that time (during the Holocaust) were killed. About 75% of all European Jews died in fact.

There simply is zero debate on this issue, and it has been completely and historically verified.

In addition to the aforementioned documentation and eyewitness accounts, the proof is there for all to see in this frightening statistic: the global Jewish population in 1939 was 15 million; today the global population of Jews is approximately 13 million.

When considering this sobering statistic, keep in mind the populations of *all* other ethnic groups increase over time. They never decrease unless there's a major famine or other natural disaster or a major conflict – or an ethnic cleansing!

Correct us if we are wrong, but outside of the Nazi purge there has been no other major event that has resulted in the deaths of millions of Jews since WW2. So if that doesn't amount to undeniable proof of the veracity of the official stats surrounding the Holocaust, we aren't sure what does.

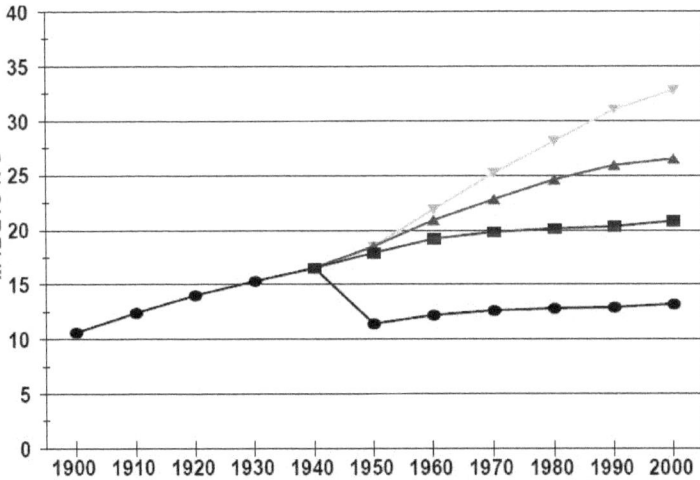

Above: Estimated Jewish World Population <u>with the Holocaust</u> (bottom line) and <u>without the Holocast</u> (top lines) occurring.

By en:Sergio DellaPergola

Book P. M. Polyzn: Otrizanie otrizaniya

Licensed under Public Domain via Wikimedia Commons

Above: *German soldier shooting a Jewish woman with a child in her arms.*

Confirmed German army mobile killing unit, Ukraine, 1942.

Public Domain

QUESTIONING THE CONFIRMED DEATH TOLL

Those stats alone should be enough to silence the doubters.

If any other ethnic group numbered 15 million in 1939, its population would ordinarily number around 25 to 30 million today. So how come the Jewish population shrunk so drastically?

The answer again is very simple and can be summed up in two words: *the Holocaust.*

"The goal of annihilating all of the Jews of Europe, as it was proclaimed at the conference in the villa Am Grossen Wannsee in January 1942, was not reached. Yet the six million murder victims make the holocaust a unique crime in the history of mankind. The number of victims — and with certainty the following represent the minimum number in each case — cannot express that adequately. Numbers are just too abstract. However they must be stated in order to make clear the dimension of the genocide: 165,000 Jews from Germany, 65,000 from Austria, 32,000 from France and Belgium, more than 100,000 from the Netherlands, 60,000 from Greece, the same number from Yugoslavia, more than 140,000 from Czechoslovakia, half a million from Hungary, 2.2 million from the Soviet Union, and 2.7 million from Poland. To these numbers must be added all those killed in the pogroms and massacres in Romania and Transitrien (over 200,000) and the deported and murdered Jews from Albania and Norway, Denmark and Italy, from Luxembourg and Bulgaria."

–Wolfgang Benz, The Holocaust: A German Historian Examines the Genocide

THREE

MYTH #2: "Three million deceased Jews in concentration camps is still a huge number. If you consider that the relentless killing didn't start until sometime into World War II, it would need an extraordinary effort for a single country which was already struggling on a two-front war. And the camps did not have the necessary infrastructure to kill and remove the bodies of millions of people. Germany did not have the logistics to pull off such a crime."

—Anonymous Holocaust denier #2

The Nazi regime's orchestration of concentration camps – labor camps, death camps, extermination camps, call them what you will – was so incredibly efficient it could serve for all time as a lesson in organization and planning. Not surprising given the Germans have long been recognized, and dare we suggest admired, for their organizational abilities.

Examples of this incredible efficiency abound, but perhaps none more graphically demonstrate this than the operation of the extermination camps – all fully documented (and fully documented by the Nazis themselves). In this respect, the Nazis' penchant for record-keeping contributed in no small way to the historical record.

There were eight major extermination camps. Each had its own modus operandi. Some, like Auschwitz, in Poland, had Zyklon B gas chambers; others, like Bełżec, also in Poland, had carbon monoxide gas chambers; still others, like Sajmište, in Serbia, and Maly Trostinets, in Belarus, used mobile gas vans instead of fixed chambers.

The highest death toll of Jewish inmates was Auschwitz at 1.1 million. That's *1,100,000* individual Jewish lives in case you missed it.

According to the Jewish Virtual Library's website, there were approximately 15,000 *known* camps, but it states, "Unfortunately, this list is far from complete" as "It does not include camps which were created for limited operations or time, as most of these were destroyed by the Nazis. Additionally, this list does not contain the names of the ghettos created by the Nazis."

The site lists the countries in which the known camps were based. These are worth noting: Austria, Belgium, Czechoslovakia, Estonia, Finland, France, Germany, Holland, Italy, Latvia, Lithuania, Norway, Poland, Russia and Yugoslavia.

Establishment of the first camps predated the commencement of WW2 by some time. For example, Dachau was established early in 1933. By 1944, it reportedly had more than 30 large sub-camps in which many thousands of prisoners were worked to death.

Research of the official records shows that collectively the camps had the necessary systems and infrastructure to easily account for the number of deaths attributed to them. The main camps at least had railway tracks right outside the gates, and untold numbers of (non-Jewish) European witnesses have reported that year in, year out, trains would arrive daily and sometimes hourly to deliver cargo. Their *cargo* mostly being men, women and children destined for the gas chambers or the labor gangs.

The book *THE TRAINS OF THE HOLOCAUST: A Study Of The Railways Transports Across Europe, During The Second [Final Phase] Of The Jewish Holocaust*, by Hedi Enghelberg, provides a detailed breakdown of just how extensive the Nazi railroad system was.

Enghelberg states, "The Nazi criminal regime (1933-1945), its military, civilian organizations, middle-level bureaucracy and associated dictatorial regimes all over Europe, succeeded in murdering millions of people and destroying a flourishing 900-years-old Jewish Culture in Europe ... An efficient railways system across the continent with more than 100,000 km of rail, (only 42,000 km of which were in Germany proper) operated by the largest private railroad at the time, the Deutsche Reichsbahn, with more than 250,000 workers and a formidable 12,500 operational locomotives (kriegslokomotiven), totally sustained and assisted Germany's formidable war machine and as aided the Nazi organizations in charge of the 'Final Solution' ... Concentration, trains transport and killing, were stories of evil forces (all over Europe) against unarmed civilian, with no chance for defense. The story is more credible, tragic and moving, because it is real and a vast majority of the transported people died on arrival (due to transport conditions) or later, in the gas chambers, in horrible conditions."

Enghelberg's book also mentions Nazi collaborators – namely the railway companies of various European nations – that made all this possible.

He explains, "The European railway companies totally and willingly assisted the Nazis in the transportation segment by carrying out this infamous crime: The Holocaust. Without the collaboration of European railways, the Holocaust could not have happened on the scale on which it did."

Anonymous Holocaust denier: for you to state it would need an extraordinary effort for a single country which was already struggling on a two-front war to kill millions of Jews reveals another common misunderstanding. The misunderstanding being that for the duration of the Holocaust, Germany was just another country.

Nazi Germany cannot be compared to modern-day Germany or to any other country for that matter because it was in fact the Third Reich – one of the most powerful empires in the history of the world.

Technologically, scientifically and in so many other ways, the Germany of that era was streets ahead of any other nation or even groups of nations.

Military historian Graeme Shimmins succinctly explains that superiority in an article on the *Quora.com* website in which he states, "The cliché is that the Germans fought the Second World War with the weapons of the fifties, whilst the Allies fought with the weapons of the thirties." He adds, "There is some truth in this."

Above: *Railway line outside the Auschwitz concentration camp.*

Credit: *By Antony Stanley from Gloucester, UK - Birkenau Tracks #1, CC BY-SA 2.0, https://commons.wikimedia.org/w/index.php?curid=28439186*

Licensed under Public Domain via Wikimedia Commons

Above: *Adolf Hitler & senior Nazi Party members in Paris, 1940.*

Note the Eiffel Tower in the background.

By Bundesarchiv, Bild 183-H28708

CC-BY-SA, CC BY-SA 3.0 de

Licensed under Public Domain via Wikimedia Commons

Shimmins reminds readers the Germans were ahead in rocketry, jet and rocket aircraft, submarines, missiles, smart bombs and small arms. "The reasons (for this) are varied," he says. "Nazi Germany had many talented scientists and engineers...German science was well funded and had a strong history. German engineering was (and still is) amongst the best in the world. The German school system was effective at churning out technicians...

"The less mass-production orientated German industry produced a wider range of equipment and moved on to new designs. German industry was also more fragmented, leading to competition to produce 'wonder weapons' in order to gain contracts... They sought to counter quantity through quality. The jet aircraft is a good example...Some of the advances were brought on by combat experience. (For example) the Stumgewehr 44 was produced after German experience revealed that volume was far more important than accuracy in most fire-fights."

The proof of Nazi Germany's scientific superiority was demonstrated at the end of WW2 when thousands of German scientists were secreted into the US as part of *Operation Paperclip*. Many of these *Paperclip Nazis* (as they came to be known) became leading figures in a number of fields, most notably in the space race and the development of rocketry. And this despite the fact that many were Nazi sympathisers and some were known war criminals whose names had to be Americanized to facilitate their assimilation into their adopted homeland. This only came to the general public's attention with the declassification of official CIA documents decades later.

Operation Paperclip, incidentally, wasn't exclusive to America. There was a three-way race between the

US, the Soviet Union and Great Britain at war's end to grab whatever German scientific expertise was available. Many German scientists ended up in Russia and Britain, and in Australia, too, albeit under different operational code names such as *Operation Matchbox* (in Britain/Australia) and *Operation Osoaviakhim* (in the Soviet Union).

Having invaded or over-run powerhouse nations like France, Austria, Belgium, Denmark, Greece and Poland, Nazi Germany looted the riches of half of Europe; it was secretly receiving funds from the Vatican Bank (and many historians believe the likes of Pope Pius XII were well aware of Hitler's intent toward the Jews) and it had the support of many Swiss banks; and of course it had the backing of its fascist allies, including Italy and Japan.

Corporate support for the Third Reich was global, blatant and widespread. To their eternal shame, numerous companies (many of them American) around the world supported the Nazis.

German engineering giant Siemens used slave labor to construct the gas chambers that became synonymous with the Holocaust. Decades after the war, the firm's consumer products joint venture Bosch Siemens Hausgeraete (BSH) made headlines for all the wrong reasons when it filed two applications to register the *Zyklon* name across a range of home products, including gas ovens – Zyklon being the name of the poison gas used in concentration camps.

A *BBC News* item dated September 5, 2002 reports, "Jewish groups have condemned the move, in particular because Siemens used slave labour during the Nazi period."

The *BBC* report continues, " 'Siemens should know better because it was directly complicit in the use of slave labour,' said Dr Shimon Samuels, head of the European arm of the Simon Wiesenthal Center, a Jewish human rights organisation. 'This is a major, major scandal'."

The report concludes, "Efforts to distribute compensation (by Siemens to victims) have been complicated by a mass of private lawsuits, mainly in US courts, alleging use of slave labour and other forms of profiteering from the Holocaust."

In his harrowing and intense memoir *Memories of Evil: Recalling a World War II Childhood*, author and Holocaust survivor Peter Kubicek describes at length how certain companies such as Siemens and others had factories attached to certain concentration camps. Kubicek, who was only in his early-mid teens during captivity and who miraculously survived six different German concentration camps because of "sheer luck" in a situation of "1000:1 odds" chances of survival, advises readers of his book these companies knew exactly what was going on and benefited greatly from the efforts of the slave laborers.

In private correspondence with us, Mr. Kubicek also advised, "The employees of Siemens never set foot in the camps. The camp prisoners worked as slave laborers in the Siemens factories. It often occurred to me that a factory like Siemens could have offered lunch to the prisoners who worked there, but that never happened: the prisoners had to march back to the camp to eat their lunch consisting of a bowl of turnip soup."

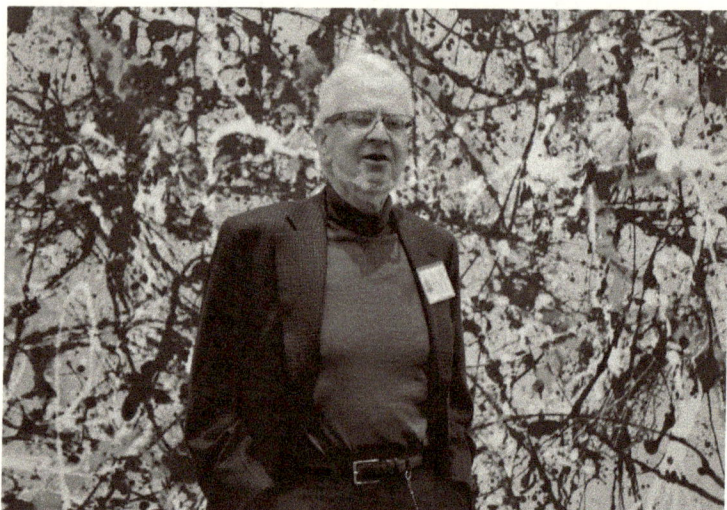

Above: *Holocaust survivor Peter Kubicek (born 1930).*

Photo courtesy of Peter Kubicek

Taken at the Metropolitan Museum of Art, New York City, NY, USA.

German multinational pharmaceutical and chemical company Bayer, known for developing aspirin, became part of chemical conglomerate IG Farben, best known as the company that profited most from working with the Nazis.

Alliance for Human Research Protection put IG Farben-Bayer in the spotlight in an article on its *AHRP.org* blog on January 27, 2005, commemorating the 60-year anniversary of Auschwitz.

Excerpts from that article follow:

"IG Farben was the most powerful German corporate cartel in the first half of the 20th century and the single largest profiteer from the Second World War...As documents show, IG Farben was intimately involved with the human experimental atrocities committed by (notorious SS officer Josef) Mengele at Auschwitz...".

The AHRP article continues, "IG Farben was the only German company in the Third Reich that ran its own concentration camp. At least 30,000 slave workers died in this camp; a lot more were deported to the gas chambers. It was no coincidence that IG Farben built their giant new plant in Auschwitz, since the workforce they used (altogether about 300,000 people) was practically for free. The Zyklon B gas, which killed millions of Jews, Gypsies and other people was produced by IG Farben´s subsidiary company Degesch.

"In Germany a growing number of people do not understand that IG Farben's successors Bayer, BASF and Hoechst still refuse to apologize for their misdeeds. It is hard to accept that after the war the companies were allowed to keep IG Farben's entire property, whereas the surviving slave workers received nothing. Until today Bayer, BASF and Hoechst did not pay any wages to their former workers."

Incidentally, the AHRP article includes harrowing interviews with Auschwitz inmates who survived medical experimentation.

An article dated September 29, 2011 in *The Telegraph* highlights the close ties that existed between the Nazis and the Quandt family empire, which became a major shareholder in German car manufacturer BMW after WW2.

Excerpts from the article follow:

" 'The Quandts were linked inseparably with the crimes of the Nazis,' concluded Joachim Scholtyseck, the Bonn historian who compiled and researched the study, 'The family patriarch was part of the regime.'

"The 1,200 page report provides details of the practises common at Quandt family factories where an estimated 50,000 slave labourers from concentration camps were used to supply arms contracts to the regime.

"Hundreds of these labourers died from working in the inhumane conditions and others were executed.

"The family was also discovered to have profited from taking over dozens of businesses seized from Jewish families by the Nazis and handed over to the Quandts."

German financial services and insurance company Allianz has the dubious distinction of having insured Auschwitz. *Wikipedia* reports, "Research concluded that Allianz, as an organization and through its corporate officers, voluntarily partnered with the Nazi Regime and the Third Reich, starting as early as the early 1930s and continuing all the way through to the collapse of the Third Reich."

According to the political and news website *11Points.com*, "Allianz has very famous Nazi ties -- they insured Auschwitz, their CEO was one of Hitler's advisers, and, during the Holocaust, instead of paying life insurance benefits to Jews, they sent that money straight to the Nazis."

The writer, incidentally, unequivocally states, "There are a TON of companies that worked with the Nazis."

German clothing manufacturer Hugo Boss is yet another company with close Nazi links. A *New York Times* article dated August 15, 1997, states, "Before Hugo Boss A.G. became known for classic men's suits and flashy ties, the clothing manufacturer made uniforms for the Nazis, a company spokeswoman acknowledged today."

The article continues, "In the 1930's, when the company began making Nazi uniforms, it was a family-run business that manufactured police and postal uniforms.

"The Nazis awarded contracts to thousands of companies to produce the black uniforms, worn by SS units, the brown shirts worn by SA storm troopers and the black-and-brown uniforms of the Hitler Youth, according to Eckhard Trox, a military uniform expert at the museum in Ludenscheid.

" 'Of course my father belonged to the Nazi Party,' Siegfried Boss, 83, said in the latest issue of the Austrian news weekly *Profil*. 'But who didn't belong back then? The whole industry worked for the Nazi Army.'

Above: Map of concentration camps in Poland alone during WW2.

By I, DenysZ, CC BY 3.0,

https://commons.wikimedia.org/w/index.php?curid=27572579

Licensed under Public Domain via Wikimedia Commons

"Hugo Boss...joined the Nazi Party in 1931, and two years later, began manufacturing Nazi uniforms. Production continued throughout the war, and according to *Profil*, the company brought forced laborers from Poland and France to its factory to increase output in the later years."

Car manufacturers Volkswagen and Porsche don't escape censure either. According to *Spiegel Online International*, both Volkswagen and Porsche had close connections with the Third Reich. An article by Dietmar Hawranek on Spiegel's website makes for interesting reading.

Excerpts from that article follow:

"Without Ferdinand Porsche, neither automotive giant Volkswagen nor luxury marque Porsche would exist today... When Hitler asked the German automobile industry to develop a 'suitable small car' in 1934, Porsche submitted the best design -- and was awarded the contract... A new factory had to be built to produce the car, as well as a new town surrounding the factory to house the workers... Only 630 Beetles were made there during World War II -- and distributed to the privileged.

"Instead, the factories were used in weapons production, to manufacture tank chains, mines and an all-terrain vehicle..."

The Spiegel article concludes, "Thousands of forced laborers were later used, including Jews from concentration camps and prisoners of war, mostly from the Soviet Union and Poland."

"The day the war ended, it appears that, in a single puff of smoke, all Nazis magically disappeared. By this extension, since all German war crimes were committed exclusively by the Nazis, once the latter disappeared, only 'us good Germans' remained. This may have been a comforting thought to the Germans, but it was, and remains, nothing but a myth. Millions of Germans clung to the belief that just a small clique of criminals bore sole responsibility for the Holocaust. The fact is that a great many ordinary Germans, soldiers, policemen, and various other groups of citizens were involved in perpetrating atrocities. And from there it was but a small further step to the myth of, 'We didn't even know.' And the world promptly swallowed this fake propaganda. From then on, through the present, we hear only about Nazi crimes in connection with the War, as in 'Nazi murderers, Nazi soldiers.' The fact is that there never was such a concept as a Nazi soldier. The German Wehrmacht was composed of a highly professional military cadre, as well as of volunteers, such as the S.S. and, of course, ordinary German conscripts. On many later occasions, when I described our torturers as Germans, I was asked whether I did not mean the Nazis. My answer is, 'Well, some of them may have been Nazis — I don't really know — but what I do know for sure is that they were Germans'."

—Peter Kubicek, *Memories of Evil: Recalling a World War II Childhood*

Prominent among the American companies that supported the Third Reich were Standard Oil, Kodak,

Coca-Cola, Ford, IBM, Random House Publishing and Chase Bank.

Chase, one of the largest American banks, is just "one of many banks that sided with the Nazis," according to the *11Points.com* site. It states, "They froze European Jewish customers' accounts and were extremely cooperative in providing banking service to Germany."

A *New York Times* article of November 7, 1998, reports, "Chase said it was also examining whether its Paris office was 'overly cooperative in providing banking services to Germany during the Occupation' and whether assets seized by the Nazis and Vichy Government were ever returned."

The article concludes, "The Clinton Administration is conducting a survey of American banks regarding their management of Jewish accounts here and abroad during World War II."

On March 29, 2002, *The Guardian* reported that "IBM dealt directly with Holocaust organisers." Excerpts from that report follow:

"Newly discovered documents from Hitler's Germany prove that the computer company IBM directly supplied the Nazis with technology which was used to help transport millions of people to their deaths in the concentration camps at Auschwitz and Treblinka, a controversial Holocaust expert claims...

"Edwin Black, whose book *IBM and the Holocaust* was published in hardback last year, says new evidence set out in the paperback version shows that executives at the firm's New York headquarters directly controlled a Polish subsidiary which leased punch-card machines used to 'calculate exactly how many Jews should be emptied out of the ghettos each day' and to transport them efficiently on railways leading to the camps."

The report continues, "When the Nazis invaded Poland, Black wrote in the Jerusalem Post, 'IBM New York established a special new subsidiary called Watson Business Machines,' after its then- president, Thomas Watson. 'IBM's new Polish company's sole purpose was to service the Nazi occupation during the rape of Poland.' Watson Business Machines even operated a punch-card printing shop over the street from the Warsaw Ghetto, the paperback claims...

"The paperback provides the first evidence that the company's dealings with the Nazis were controlled from its New York headquarters throughout the second world war... The company (IBM), now based in Armonk in upper New York state, has not denied the role of its subsidiaries in aiding the Nazis' management of the Holocaust, preferring to suggest that it should not be held responsible for the actions of companies of which the Third Reich had seized control."

The Guardian report concludes, "Mr Black cites numerous examples of stories in US newspapers at the time which he says should have left IBM in no doubt about the nature of the Nazis' murderous activities in Poland."

Technology company Kodak is another American company with a dubious past. On March 26, 2001, *The Nation* reported the following:

"New information recently uncovered at the National Archives reveals that subsidiaries of the Eastman Kodak company traded with Nazi Germany long after America had entered the war. A number of US firms have been identified previously as having been involved with the Nazi regime; most recently IBM was cited in a lawsuit filed in early February."

The article continues, "The archive documents also provide a glimpse of the attitudes of some US and British government officials during that period who were unwilling to impose any sanctions against the firm, recommending instead that Kodak continue trading to preserve its market position...

"Kodak's revenues and employees in Germany increased during the early years of the war as the company expanded to manufacture triggers, detonators and other military hardware... In Germany Kodak used slave laborers, according to Fings and Roland Wig of the Milberg Weiss law firm, which has been active in Holocaust-related lawsuits. At Kodak's Stuttgart plant, there were at least eighty slave laborers, and at the Berlin-Kopenick factory there were more than 250 slave laborers."

The Nation article concludes, "a related subject, Professor Saul Friedlander, the historian who chairs the commission investigating Bertelsmann's Nazi past, said that a final report, which could be as long as 500 pages, is expected to be released by the end of the year."

Legendary anti-Semite Henry Ford, founder of the Ford Motor Company, had a well-deserved reputation for being Hitler's most famous foreign backer. An article on the *Reformed-Theology.org* blog puts this into perspective:

"Henry Ford was also the most famous of Hitler's foreign backers, and he was rewarded in the 1930s for this long-lasting support with the highest Nazi decoration for foreigners.

"This Nazi favor aroused a storm of controversy in the United States and ultimately degenerated into an exchange of diplomatic notes between the German Government and the State Department. While Ford publicly protested that he did not like totalitarian governments, we find in practice that Ford knowingly profited from both sides of World War II — from French and German plants producing vehicles at a profit for the Wehrmacht, and from U.S. plants building vehicles at a profit for the U.S. Army."

The article continues, "Henry Ford's protestations of innocence suggest...that he did not approve of Jewish financiers profiting from war (as some have), but if anti-Semitic Morgan and Ford profited from war that was acceptable, moral and 'constructive.'

"On December 20, 1922 the *New York Times* reported that...Ford was financing Adolph Hitler's nationalist and anti-Semitic movements in Munich. Simultaneously, the Berlin newspaper *Berliner Tageblatt* appealed to the American Ambassador in Berlin to investigate and halt Henry Ford's intervention into German domestic affairs. It was reported that Hitler's foreign backers had furnished a 'spacious headquarters' with a 'host of highly paid lieutenants and officials.' Henry Ford's portrait was prominently displayed on the walls of Hitler's personal office...

"In August 1938...Ford received the Grand Cross of the German Eagle, a Nazi decoration for distinguished foreigners. The New York Times reported it was the first time the Grand Cross had been awarded in the United States and was to celebrate Henry Ford's 75th birthday."

Above: *Henry Ford accepts the Grand Cross of the Supreme Order of the German Eagle for invaluable contributions to the Third Reich.*

Public Domain Image

Above: *Dr Fritz Klein, camp doctor and convicted war criminal, standing in a mass grave at the Belsen concentration camp.*

Licensed under Public Domain via Wikimedia Commons

If you didn't already know, you will be aware by now that numerous American companies supported the Third Reich, and their support either directly or indirectly impacted upon Europe's Jews. Other major American companies not mentioned thus far are listed on the *TopTenz.net* website and include: Metro-Goldwyn-Mayer, Dow Chemical, Brown Brothers Harriman, Woolworth, Alcoa and General Motors.

So, Anonymous Holocaust denier, rather than questioning whether Nazi Germany had the necessary infrastructure and logistics to kill and remove the bodies of millions of people, a more appropriate question would be: *Could a regime that controlled most of Europe's resources and wealth, and had the backing of many of the world's biggest corporations, kill a few million defenceless Jews?*

The obvious answer is: Yes! Most certainly!

Even during Yugoslavia's relatively small-scale Balkan/Bosnian wars in the 1990s, ethnic killings claimed tens of thousands of lives. The images of the mass graves unearthed in the aftermath of those comparatively minor conflicts (minor compared to WW2) were for many a flashback to the genocide that was the Holocaust. Commentators around the world observed that, sadly, the lessons of the past had apparently not been learned.

"Hitler exterminated the Jews of Europe. But he did not do so alone. The task was so enormous, complex, time-consuming, and mentally and economically demanding that it took the best efforts of millions of Germans... All spheres of life in Germany actively participated: Businessmen, policemen,

bankers, doctors, lawyers, soldiers, railroad and factory workers, chemists, pharmacists, foremen, production managers, economists, manufacturers, jewelers, diplomats, civil servants, propagandists, film makers and film stars, professors, teachers, politicians, mayors, party members, construction experts, art dealers, architects, landlords, janitors, truck drivers, clerks, industrialists, scientists, generals, and even shopkeepers—all were essential cogs in the machinery that accomplished the final solution."

–Konnilyn G. Feig, *Hitler's death camps: the sanity of madness*

FOUR

VERIFYING THE GAS CHAMBER EXTERMINATIONS

MYTH #3: "Many Jews died in the camps as a result of harsh conditions, starvation, illness and disease as opposed to being gassed. That assertion doesn't make the end result any more tenable, but it does undermine the supposed history of the Holocaust."

—Anonymous Holocaust denier #3

Um...no. The fact that some of the three million who died in the concentration camps were killed by other means (besides gassing) does not remotely undermine Holocaust history. The gassings were simply one cause of the deaths, and nobody has ever suggested all those who died in the camps were gassed. Certainly, most were gassed, but not all.

Remember, the camps were not only designed to exterminate Jews and others deemed undesirable. They also served as labor camps whose inmates were often literally worked to death to support Germany's war effort and help meet the insatiable needs of the Third Reich. And Nazi scientists conducted wide-scale medical experimentation on hundreds of thousands of victims inside the camps – horrific experiments, which few survived.

One of a frightening number of examples of influential people making statements *against* the historicity of the extermination camps and gas chambers is Lutheran pastor Herman Otten, who, at the Ninth IHR (Institute for Historical Review) Conference in 1989, made the following claim:

"There is no dispute over the fact that large numbers of Jews were deported to concentration camps and ghettos, or that many Jews died or were killed during World War II. Revisionist scholars have presented evidence, which 'exterminationists' have not been able to refute, showing that there was no German program to exterminate Europe's Jews, and that the estimate of six million Jewish wartime dead is an irresponsible exaggeration. The Holocaust – the alleged extermination of some six million Jews (most of them by gassing) – is a hoax and should be recognized as such by Christians and all informed, honest and truthful men everywhere."

Another example of deniers stating the gas chambers are a myth was reported by German media outlet *DW News* on April 16, 2010. The article reported that "Ultra-conservative bishop Richard Williamson has been fined 10,000 euros for denying aspects of the Holocaust in an interview for Swedish television. He made the comments while on German soil."

During the televised interview, the British Roman Catholic Bishop stated, "I believe that the historical evidence is strongly against, is hugely against, six million Jews having been deliberately gassed in gas chambers as a deliberate policy of Adolf Hitler."

Above: *Starved prisoners in the Ebensee concentration camp in Austria.*

The camp was reputedly used for "scientific" experiments.

U.S. National Archives and Records Administration

Licensed under Public Domain via Wikimedia Commons

Williamson added, "I think that 200,000 to 300,000 Jews perished in Nazi concentration camps, but none of them in gas chambers."

Another denier, claiming to be neutral, wrote to us on social media with this curious comment: "We know for a fact that great numbers of Jews were rounded up and taken to camps, and that great numbers of them died there. But beyond these clear facts, it starts to get more blurry. There may be indications that these were primarily intended as purely work camps. During WW2 all the belligerent powers were short of labor, so that actually makes more sense. There are also problems with the evidence for gas chambers."

On the contrary, there is an abundance of evidence for the gas chambers. That is why all mainstream historians agree the chambers are 100% verified and that a large percentage of those who died in the camps died from the result of either carbon monoxide or Zyklon B gas poisoning.

A good summary of the historically-proven facts about the gas chambers can be found on the Jewish Virtual Library site in an article headed "Gassing Victims in the Holocaust." Skeptics be advised all of these facts have been confirmed in Nazi documentation no less, examples of which can be found later in this chapter.

Meanwhile, here's a relevant excerpt from the Jewish Virtual Library:

"The systematic murdering of humans through gas during the Nazi rule was introduced for the first time from January 1940 on in the area of the 'Euthanasia', the extermination of the 'lives not worthy to live' of the handicapped, mental patients and the terminally ill,

Above: *Empty Zyklon B gas canisters found at Auschwitz in 1945.*

Image taken from Auschwitz II museum showcase.

Licensed under Public Domain via Wikimedia Commons

Above: *Hole above one of Auschwitz's gas chambers used by the Nazis to throw granulated crystal Zyklon B.*

By Lasy - Own work, CC BY-SA 4.0,

https://commons.wikimedia.org/w/index.php?curid=40107910

Licensed under Public Domain via Wikimedia Commons

and from fall 1941 on was continued to a much larger extent by the pogroms of the operation groups of the security police and the SD in the seized eastern areas with the help of mobile gas vans.

"Beginning December of 1941 one proceeded in the camp Kulmhof (Polish Chelmno) to use stationary gas vans for the killing of Jews, and from the beginning of 1942 in different camps fixed gas chambers were built, or already existing buildings were restructured for this purpose."

The article also makes an important distinction. "One needs to differentiate by the furnishing of such gas chambers and the gassing actions carried out within them between the mass gassings of Jews in the extermination camps built for that purpose and the gassings of smaller scale in individual, already existing concentration camps (whereby patients, seized forced laborers, war prisoners, and political prisoners among others were also victims)."

As mentioned, the Nazis themselves left sufficient documentation to verify the large-scale usage of gas chambers in the camps. This despite their efforts to destroy documentation and other evidence late in the war when they realized all was lost, and despite their determination to conceal the extent of the Holocaust from the German public.

The examples (of Nazi verification of the gas chamber exterminations) are too many to list, but here's a few for the record:

A 1943 letter written by Auschwitz head architect Karl Bischoff ordered "three gas tight doors" for Crema 3 following "exactly the size and construction of those already delivered" for Crema 2." Bischoff's urgently-marked letter, which was addressed to the German

Armament Works, specified the doors needed a spy-hole of double 8-mm glass "with a rubber seal and metal fitting."

The Korherr Report is another strong piece of evidence. Written in March, 1943, by SS doctor Richard Korherr, it states 2.5 million European Jews had been "evacuated" for "special treatment." (Note that the phrase *special treatment* is a coded Nazi term WW2 historians commonly agree refers to genocide within the camps, especially via gas chambers).

The Höfle Telegram, which was written in 1943 and discovered in 2000, is one of the few Nazi documents found that mentions and describes *Operation Reinhard*, the codename given to the top-secret German plan to mass-murder Polish Jews in Polish concentration camps.

SS-Officer Rudolf Höss, the longest-serving commandant of Auschwitz concentration camp, testified after WW2 that it was possible to kill 2,000 people per hour via the Zyklon B gas he introduced to the camp: "Technically [it] wasn't so hard—it would not have been hard to exterminate even greater numbers.... The killing itself took the least time. You could dispose of 2,000 head in half an hour, but it was the burning that took all the time. The killing was easy; you didn't even need guards to drive them into the chambers; they just went in expecting to take showers and, instead of water, we turned on poison gas. The whole thing went very quickly."

Heinrich Himmler, Reichsführer of the Schutzstaffel (Protection Squadron, SS), and one of the most senior and influential members of the Nazi Party, not only explicitly described the mass extermination of Jews that was underway in a speech he gave to other

German officers on October 4th, 1943, in the city of Posen (now Poland), but also stated the genocide needed to be kept a total secret and never recorded.

Here are the relevant excerpts of Himmler's 1943 speech as recorded in the *Office of the United States Chief of Counsel For Prosecution of Axis Criminality*, and as translated (from German into English) by the Nizkor Project. (Note that recovered Nazi audio recordings of this wartime speech are all over the internet for anyone to freely listen to):

"I also want to talk to you, quite frankly, on a very grave matter. Among ourselves it should be mentioned quite frankly, and yet we will never speak of it publicly. Just as we did not hesitate on June 30th, 1934 to do the duty we were bidden, and stand comrades who had lapsed, up against the wall and shoot them, so we have never spoken about it and will never speak of it. It was that tact which is a matter of course and which I am glad to say, is inherent in us, that made us never discuss it among ourselves, never to speak of it. It appalled everyone, and yet everyone was certain that he would do it the next time if such orders are issued and if it is necessary – I mean the clearing out of the Jews, the extermination of the Jewish race. ... Most of you must know what it means when 100 corpses are lying side by side, or 500 or 1,000 ... This is a page of glory in our history which has never been written and is never to be written."

The World Holocaust Remembrance Center, Yad Vashem, lists an eyewitness account by SS Non-commissioned officer (SS-Unterscharführer) Perry Broad, who served at Auschwitz from 1942–1945.

In the following, Broad describes an occasion he witnessed Jews being murdered within one of Auschwitz's gas chambers:

"A number of victims noticed that the covers had been removed from the six holes in the ceiling (of the gas chamber). They screamed in terror when a head, covered in a gas-mask, appeared at one of the holes. The 'disinfectors' went to work... Using a hammer and chisel, they opened some innocuous-looking tins which bore the inscription 'Zyklon, to be used against vermin. Attention, poison! To be opened by trained personnel only.' As soon as the tins were opened, their contents were thrown through the holes, and the covers were replaced immediately... about two minutes later, the screams died down, and only muffled groans could be heard. Most of the victims had already lost consciousness. Two more minutes passed, and Grabner (one of the SS men) stopped looking at his watch. Absolute silence prevailed."

"In nature life always takes measures against parasites; in the life of nations that is not always the case. From this fact the Jewish peril actually stems. There is therefore no other recourse left for modern nations except to exterminate the Jew."

–Joseph Goebbels, Reich Minister of Propaganda in Nazi Germany

Testimonies confirming the existence of the gas chambers and the dreadful use they were put to have also been given by untold numbers of concentration camp survivors, by workers whose number include railroad crews, and by 'corpse disposal prisoners' known as *Sonderkommandos* who were tasked with disposing of the bodies of gassed victims and who, day after day, witnessed first-hand the extermination campaign; and last but not least are those German officers and guards whose post-war testimonials and confessions provide further proof.

Even the Allies expressed awareness of the Holocaust fairly early on in WW2.

For example, in December 1942, Britain's Foreign Minister Anthony Eden condemned the ongoing mass murder of Jews after reading the *Joint Declaration by Members of the United Nations* drafted by the American and British governments on behalf of the Allied Powers.

Eden mentioned the "numerous reports from Europe that the German authorities, not content with denying to persons of Jewish race in all the territories over which their barbarous rule has been extended, the most elementary human rights, are now carrying into effect Hitler's oft-repeated intention to exterminate the Jewish people in Europe. From all the occupied countries Jews are being transported in conditions of appalling horror and brutality to Eastern Europe. In Poland, which has been made the principal Nazi slaughterhouse, the ghettos established by the German invader are being systematically emptied of all Jews except a few highly skilled workers required for war industries. None of those taken away are ever heard of again. The able-bodied are slowly worked to death in labor camps. The infirm are left to die of exposure and starvation or are deliberately massacred in mass executions."

"I would like you to believe me. I saw the gas chambers. I saw the crematoria. I saw the open fires. I was on the ramp when the selections took place. I would like you to believe that these atrocities happened because I was there."

–Oskar Gröning, former member of the SS stationed at Auschwitz concentration camp

Now, the cornerstone of almost every Holocaust denier's argument is the gas chambers – or, as they mischievously insist, *the lack of* gas chambers.

You'll recall David Irving's comment (quoted in chapter 1) about the Auschwitz gas chambers being as genuine as Disneyland. Unfortunately, he's not alone in his belief. The deniers regularly trot out "evidence" in the form of erroneous information to attempt to prove their theory that the Nazis' gas chambers either did not exist or were used for delousing or for other reasons that had nothing to do with the mass murders of human beings. Unsubstantiated theories all easily disproven.

Very few Holocaust deniers are scientists, and yet they insist on repeating scientific myths that have been debunked numerous times.

Common myths include:

- Hydrogen cyanide (in the form of Zyklon B) is either too explosive to use or else cannot be used to exterminate humans.
- There was no Prussian Blue (a sure sign of Zyklon B usage) on the gas chamber walls.
- Gas chambers are too difficult to ventilate.
- It's not possible to kill millions of people in gas chambers in the course of a few years.

Above: *Auschwitz I gas chamber memorial.*
By Black Stripe at English Wikipedia
CC BY-SA 3.0
Licensed under Public Domain via Wikimedia Commons

Above: *Reinforced concrete gas chamber at Majdanek.*
Note the <u>Prussian Blue</u> on the walls from the Zyklon B.
Credit: By Cezary p - Own work, GFDL,
Licensed under Public Domain via Wikimedia Commons

Given Holocaust deniers and all those with an irrational hatred of Jews cannot win any sane historical argument, and given the public (generally) have little scientific understanding, it's not surprising deniers resort to using "scientific speak" to recruit followers to their erroneous belief systems.

Leftover cans of Zyklon B were found all over Nazi-occupied Europe after WW2. New York's *The Algemeiner* newspaper mentions this in an April 2015 article titled "Holocaust Denial is Real – and Frightening."

An excerpt from the article follows:

"Everyone – except the idiots of the world – knows the truth about Auschwitz-Birkenau, the largest of the Nazi death camps, and the one where an estimated 1.3 million people were murdered. It is preserved as it was in January 1945 when the camp was liberated. The gas chambers at Birkenau were destroyed by the Nazis to remove evidence of their atrocities. But the reminders of the horrors are the plentiful human hair, shoes, suitcases, and eyeglasses of the victims. Above all, there are the empty canisters of Zyklon B poison, and evidence of documentation of the Nazi planning of the genocide, mostly – at least 90 percent – against Jews."

When it comes to the actual usage of Zyklon B, deniers *are* correct in that it was originally created and used as a delousing agent in the concentration camps, but that does not disprove or diminish the fact that Zyklon B was also used to exterminate people.

To this day, the walls of one of the gas chambers at the Majdanek extermination camp (*pictured above*) – a site the Nazis failed to even partly destroy – has the tell-tale strong blue coloring that occurs when the cyanide fumes of Zyklon B react with iron.

As for hydrogen cyanide being too explosive to use, this is directly refuted by the Nazis themselves in their own literature regarding Zyklon B.

Nuremberg document NI-9912 reads: "Danger of explosion: 75 grams of HCN in 1 cubic meter of air. Normal application approx. 8-10 grams per cubic meter, therefore not explosive."

The Nizkor Project, a venture run by B'nai B'rith Canada, which is dedicated to countering Holocaust denial, consulted scientists on Zyklon B and concluded: "There would have been no real danger of explosion even if there were a bonfire burning in the gas chamber while the execution was taking place."

The use of poisonous gas to exterminate people predated the Holocaust. According to French historian Claude Ribbe, in the 19th Century Napoleon used sulfur dioxide in the enclosed holds of ships. In his book *Le Crime de Napoléon*, Ribbe reports up to 100,000 rebellious slaves were executed in these makeshift maritime gas chambers.

And the idea that gas chambers cannot be used to exterminate people is directly contradicted by their usage in the US where for decades they were used to carry out the death penalty in many states. In fact, gas chambers were built to exterminate prisoners in America from the 1920s onwards.

Mobile gas vans were invented in the Soviet Union. These Soviet gas vans, which the Nazis utilized later in the Holocaust, were used from 1936 onwards and were disguised as bread vans.

In more recent times, there have been reports of gas chambers being used to exterminate innocent people

Above: *A gas chamber at New Mexico Penitentiary, Santa Fe.*
B By Shelka04 at en.wikipedia, CC BY 3.0,
Licensed under Public Domain via Wikimedia Commons

in North Korea. On February 1, 2004, *The Guardian* reported that "horrific chemical experiments" were being "conducted on human beings" in this militant republic.

Sobering excerpts from *The Guardian* article follow. (Note we have italicised references to gas chambers):

"In the remote north-eastern corner of North Korea...is Haengyong...This remote town is home to Camp 22 - North Korea's largest concentration camp, where thousands of men, women and children accused of political crimes are held.

"Now, it is claimed, it is also where thousands die each year and where prison guards stamp on the necks of babies born to prisoners to kill them.

"Over the past year harrowing first-hand testimonies from North Korean defectors have detailed execution and torture, and now chilling evidence has emerged that the walls of Camp 22 hide an even more evil secret: *gas chambers where horrific chemical experiments are conducted on human beings.*

"Witnesses have described watching *entire families being put in glass chambers and gassed.* They are left to an agonising death while scientists take notes."

Witnesses quoted in the above article include a "former military attaché at the North Korean Embassy in Beijing" who, the writer claims, "was also the chief of management at Camp 22."

Vast amounts of physical evidence of the genocide that was the Holocaust have been recovered from the Nazi concentration camps. These include mass graves – uncovered at Treblinka, Sobibor and Auschwitz to name but three – the remains of human bodies inside and outside the camps, swathes of ash containing hair, bones, teeth and other body parts, and shoes, suitcases, eyeglasses, prosthetics and other personal belongings left behind by the victims. And, of course, there are the various examples of recovered extermination equipment – including the gas chambers themselves.

Crucially, much of this material has undergone independent forensic examination that further verifies the Holocaust.

Perhaps the most poignant item of evidence confirming the horrific numbers of victims the gas chambers claimed is the victims' shoes. You will know what we are talking about if you've seen those unforgettable photographs of mountainous piles of discarded shoes – big and pathetically small.

The Soviets recovered 300,000 pairs of shoes from the Auschwitz and Majdanek camps alone. Some 20,000 pairs of adults' and children's shoes are estimated to have been collected daily during the exterminations, which matches the reported rate of gassings at Auschwitz.

Now, either the Nazis collected shoes to indulge a bizarre shoe fetish, or these shoes belonged to the innocents they murdered...

No points for guessing which is infinitely more likely to be true!

Besides all this physical evidence regarding the Nazis' extermination measures, the universal post-war findings of historians, the testimonies from survivors and eyewitnesses, and the official documents and statements from the Nazis themselves, there have been numerous independent scientific reports on the actual gas chambers.

Above: *A pile of shoes after the liberation of the Majdanek camp (1945).*

Public domain image

French pharmacist and former Holocaust denier Jean Claude Pressac initiated a forensic examination of the Auschwitz gas chambers in 1979. He was stunned when the verdict provided overwhelming scientific evidence confirming the chambers' usage. A decade later, Pressac published a book in which he conceded that not only were Auschwitz's gas chambers functional, but they were used to exterminate more than 700,000 people.

A thorough 1994 scientific study by the Polish Government revealed that "in spite of the passage of a considerable period of time (over 45 years) in the walls of the facilities which once were in contact with hydrogen cyanide the vestigial amounts of the combinations of this constituent of Zyklon B had been preserved. This is also true of the ruins of the former gas chambers."

An article published on *Quora* and written by skeptic and historian Tim O'Neill, does an excellent job at outlining other scientific evidence for the Nazi extermination program including their gas chambers.

Titled "Is there physical scientific proof that Jews were gassed to death in Nazi concentration camps?", O'Neill answers, "Firstly, we have archaeological evidence. While the Nazis tried to cover up their crimes by destroying the evidence of gas chambers and the other killing apparatus, blowing up the chambers and crematoria at Auschwitz-Bikenau for example, there is still solid evidence that corroborates the eye-witness accounts. Careful examination of the ruins of the Crematoria I and II gas chambers at Auschwitz and comparison with photographs and descriptions from witnesses confirms the existence of the holes in the roofs of the chambers by which the Zyklon B gas pellets were introduced. Holocaust deniers claim these holes don't exist and that these structures were not gas chambers, but examination of the ruins shows that the holes in question were in place before the attempted demolition of the chambers and were not the result of that action.

"Between 2010 and 2012 a British archaeological team uncovered extensive evidence that the Treblinka camp was indeed a mass murder centre. Ground penetrating radar detected three huge mass graves on the site, one of which is 26m (26 meters or 85 feet) long, 17m wide and at least 4m deep. Using aerial photos from the 1940s, GPS technology and modern remote sensing equipment, the archaeologists were also able to detect the brick remains of the gas chambers, which the Nazis had dismantled when they abandoned the site. Bone fragments and ash deposits on the site also clearly indicate the disposal of thousands of corpses at Treblinka, as attested by all witnesses.

"Secondly," O'Neill concludes, "we have forensic evidence that clearly demonstrates that cyanide gas was used in the gas chambers at Auschwitz-Birkenau. Following claims by amateur hobbyist Fred Leuchter, which were touted by Holocaust deniers David Irving and Ernst Zundel as "proof" no Zyklon B was used to gas people at Auschwitz, the Institute for Forensic Research (IFRC) in Kraków undertook forensic examinations of the relevant areas of the five crematoria. After factoring in elements that Leuchter had not calculated for, the IFRC concluded that, in fact, there were expected traces of cyanide gas in all relevant areas and that this was not due to them having been fumigated against a typhus outbreak."

Confirmation of the existence and usage of the gas chambers in the genocide of the Jews also passed the ultimate test in a court of law.

The aforementioned Holocaust denier David Irving attempted to sue American historian Deborah E. Lipstadt over comments she made about him in her book *Denying the Holocaust: The Growing Assault on Truth and Memory*. The UK libel case, known as *Irving v Penguin Books and Lipstadt*, was won by Lipstadt – and, more importantly, the case used extensive forensic examination of the gas chambers to disprove Irving's Holocaust denial theories.

It's worth noting that during this case, which occurred at the High Court of Justice in London, Judge Gray completely dismissed Irving's claims that the Nazi gas chambers were an historic and scientific impossibility, by saying the "cumulative effect of the documentary evidence for the genocidal operation of the gas chambers" was not only "considerable" but also "mutually corroborative."

Judge Gray also noted the eyewitness accounts and documentary evidence was "striking[ly]...consistent" and concluded that "no objective, fair-minded historian would have serious cause to doubt" the existence and wide-scale usage of the gas chambers at Auschwitz.

In summary, Judge Gray found Irving's arguments to be "perverse and egregious" and also stated that Irving had "significantly misrepresented what the evidence, objectively examined, reveals."

In his book, *Lying About Hitler: History, Holocaust And The David Irving Trial*, Sir Richard J. Evans, a Cambridge historian and the chief advisor for the defense in the Irving v Penguin Books and Lipstadt case, wrote: "Not one of Irving's books, speeches or articles, not one paragraph, not one sentence in any of them, can be taken on trust as an accurate representation of its historical subject. All of them are completely worthless as history, because Irving cannot be trusted anywhere, in any of them, to give a reliable account of what he is talking or writing about."

There have been other court cases over the years that have used historical and scientific evidence to prove the historicity of *every facet of* the Holocaust as told by mainstream historians.

For example, in 1981, the notoriously anti-Semitic Institute for Historical Review (IHR) and its founder Willis Carto suffered a significant reversal as a result of a lawsuit filed by attorney William John Cox on behalf of his client, Auschwitz survivor Mel Mermelstein. *Newsweek* and other media outlets reported that after painstakingly analyzing Carto's and the IHR's denial arguments, as well as scholarly evidence relating to Auschwitz and its multiple gas chambers, the court took "judicial notice of the fact that Jews were gassed to death at Auschwitz Concentration Camp in Poland during the summer of 1944." The court concluded that "It is simply a fact."

"Deniers have said for years that physical evidence is lacking because they have seen no holes in the roof of the Birkenau gas chamber where the Zyklon was poured in. (In some of the gas chambers the Zyklon B was poured in through the roof, while in others it was thrown in through the windows.) The roof was dynamited at war's end, and today lies broken in pieces, but three of the four original holes were positively identified in a recent paper.

Their location in the concrete matches with
eyewitness testimony, aerial photos from 1944,
and a ground photo from 1943. The physical
evidence shows unmistakably that the Zyklon
holes were cast into the concrete when the
building was constructed."

–Deborah Lipstadt, Denying the Holocaust (BBC
History article)

There is one final point we need to make in relation
to the purposeful misrepresentation of facts
surrounding the Holocaust. This being it is a common
mistake for newcomers (to the Holocaust) to be
swayed by deniers who fail to alert them to the fact that
most of the remaining gas chambers are not in the
same state they were during WW2 – a detail that is
universally agreed on (by those in the know at least).

It is indisputable that some gas chambers, including
those at Auschwitz, were in such a state of disrepair
they had to be rebuilt if they were to be preserved for
posterity. Majdanek, in Poland, is one of the only death
camps remaining in its WW2 state. Its gas chambers
are wholly intact. Others, including Treblinka and
Sobibór, were completely destroyed, and still more
were partially destroyed.

Unfortunately, this is not the most widely reported
fact to come out of the Holocaust. In many ways, it's a
forgotten fact. We have even come across some
reasonably experienced Holocaust researchers who
did not realize Auschwitz's gas chambers, for example,
are primarily reconstructions of the originals that were
in the main destroyed by the Nazis.

Holocaust deniers and anti-Semites of course love
to play on this confusion, pointing out any anomalies

Above: *A photo of Auschwitz–Birkenau concentration camp, taken by an American surveillance plane, 13 September 1944.*

(Note the gas chambers II & III and IV&V near top).

Credit: U.S. National Archives and Records Administration, Licensed under Public Domain via Wikimedia Commons.

that may exist in research concerning the gas chambers. One example being what remains of the chambers at Auschwitz have no obvious or easily detected signs that Zyklon-B gas was deployed within them. (Not obvious to the naked eye at least as it is at Majdanek where you can find the tell-tale blue-stained walls resulting from the Zyklon B gassings).

When quoting this Auschwitz example, the deniers mischievously overlook the fact that the chambers are not remotely in the same condition they were during WW2 when the exterminations took place. More to the point, *some* are not even the same chambers, realistic and authentic though they may be.

Also in the case of the Auschwitz chambers, deniers overlook, or, perhaps more to the point, fail to report that forensic testing by the aforementioned IFRC revealed Zyklon B gas was definitely used in this camp's chambers.

An illustration of twisting this underreported factor of reconstructed gas chambers into supposed evidence of a hoax can be found in a February 1995 issue of the Japanese magazine *Marco Polo*. That issue published a Holocaust denial piece, written by Doctor Masanori Nishioka, which stated: "The 'Holocaust' is a fabrication. There were no execution gas chambers in Auschwitz or in any other concentration camp. Today, what are displayed as 'gas chambers' at the remains of the Auschwitz camp in Poland are a post-war fabrication by the Polish communist regime or by the Soviet Union, which controlled the country. Not once, neither at Auschwitz nor in any territory controlled by the Germans during the Second World War, was there 'mass murder of Jews' in 'gas chambers'."

The fact that most of the chambers are not in their original state all goes back once again to the Nazis partly or completely dismantling concentration camps, and removing the remains of the deceased, to hide as much evidence as possible that millions had been exterminated.

One example of this was a top-secret Nazi order for the dismantling of the camps. Known as *Sonderaktion 1005*, which translates to *Special Action 1005*, it was a special order to conceal evidence of all murders by Nazi Germany in occupied Poland. Conducted in almost total secrecy, the Sonderaktion 1005 forced prisoners to unearth mass graves and burn the bodies. These prisoners were known as *Leichenkommandos*, which means *corpse units*.

Late in the war, the Nazis focused on destroying all evidence of the Holocaust, or the worst of it at least, which of course was the gas chambers in the concentration camps. Commandos dismantled the camps, and the gas chambers, records and documentation were (mostly) systematically destroyed.

However, as alluded to earlier, the one camp the Nazis could not reach in time was Majdanek. This Polish extermination camp would have been completely dismantled were it not for the advancing Soviet Red Army who arrived in time to prevent its destruction.

As a result, SS Officer Anton Thernes, deputy commandant of administration at Majdanek, could offer little defence when he was later prosecuted for war crimes, and the gas chambers at the camp remain one of the most intact examples of the Nazis' hideous extermination facilities.

Above & Below: *Corpses of gas victims waiting to be burned at Auschwitz.*

Note original photo (above) is framed by a gas chamber's doorway or window.

Photo taken By Alberto "Alex" Errera, a member of the Sonderkommando from Greece, who died in Auschwitz in 1944.

Licensed under Public Domain via Wikimedia Commons

Above: *A Sonderkommando 1005 unit pose next to a bone-crushing machine in the Janowska camp.*

Photo by anonymous "SS officer" of Janowska concentration camp

U.S. Holocaust Memorial Museum - ushmm.org

Licensed under Public Domain via Wikimedia Commons

Above: *One of the destroyed gas chambers at Auschwitz.*
By Joshua Doubek - Own work, CC BY-SA 3.0,
Licensed under Public Domain via Wikimedia Commons

Above: *Naked women at Auschwitz being marched to gas chambers.*

Licensed under Public Domain via Wikimedia Commons

Above: *Nazi blueprints of the Crematorium II gas chamber at Auschwitz.*

Licensed under Public Domain via Wikimedia Commons

FIVE

MYTH #4: "We now know media and governments lie and that all wars are made by propaganda. They lied a lot about Hitler, even silly things like saying he was a paedophile, he had only one testicle, he had flatulence, etc. If they lied or exaggerated about such things, how can we be certain the rest of the things they told us about World War Two are absolutely true? I am pretty sure Hitler had racist ideas and saw Jewry as his main enemy. However, his main objective was NOT to wipe out the Jews from the face of the Earth. If they had departed from Germany it would have been reasonable for him."

—*Anonymous Holocaust denier #4*

Let's face it, wars generate lots of propaganda. Always have, always will, and all participants are guilty of it. As the Greek dramatist Aeschylus (525 BC - 456BC) wrote, "In war, truth is the first casualty."

Rarely does propaganda have a lot to do with reality. Even less so in wartime or when sowing the seeds of war – WW2 and the build-up to it being a case in point.

In the case of Adolf Hitler, speculation and tittle-tattle about his private life are not remotely related to how many Jews died in the Holocaust. To believe otherwise is like saying just because racist wartime cartoons compared the Japanese to animals, and even accused them of bestiality, that proves they didn't kill many millions throughout Asia and the Pacific in WW2. The historical records, of course, conclusively show the Japanese did kill that many.

The bottom line is Hitler's intentions toward the Jews are *not* in question.

If you read *Mein Kampf* and listen to Hitler's speeches, exterminating the Jews was a major part of his agenda. Nazi Germany's desire for 'racial purity' was very real, and the concepts and aims of the *Final Solution* (the Nazi policy of annihilating Jews) are well documented.

Did Hitler also have world domination and other wider goals not related to exterminating Jews? Yes most definitely, but that doesn't change the fact his expressed desire to eliminate these people, and to expel them not only from Germany but from the ever-expanding Third Reich, is all on-the-record and official.

No getting around that fact.

One of the earliest deniers to promote the idea that Hitler never specified for Jews to be exterminated was Harry Elmer Barnes (1889–1968) – a mainstream American historian who devolved into a "Holocaust revisionist" in his later years and became one of the godfathers of the denial movement.

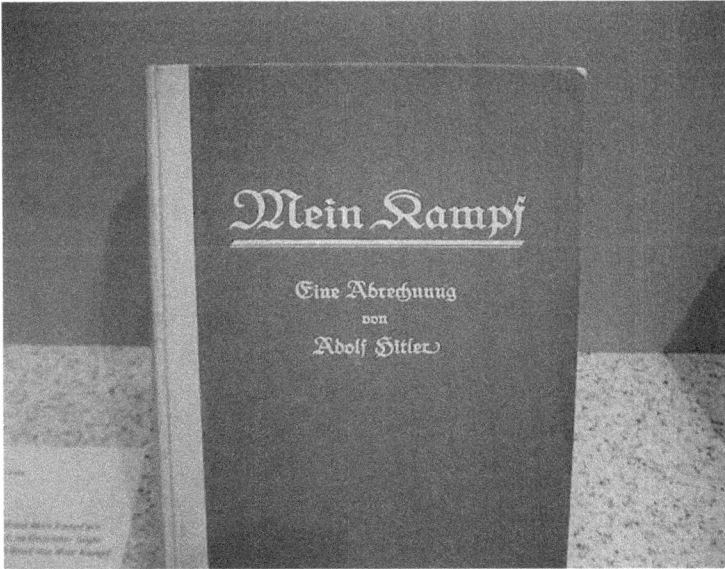

Above: *First edition of Adolf Hitler's book "Mein Kampf"*
(July, 1925).

By Anton Huttenlocher - Own photograph

Licensed under Public Domain via Wikimedia Commons

And one of numerous examples of Barnes' attempts to shift responsibility away from Hitler are to be found in this quote attributed to him in Deborah Lipstadt's book *Denying the Holocaust: The Growing Assault on Truth and Memory*. (Note the key words we've italicised):

"The size of the German reparations to Israel has been based on the *theory* that vast numbers of Jews were exterminated at the *express order of Hitler*, some six million being the most usually accepted number."

In other words, Barnes is saying there's no evidence Hitler ordered the extermination of Jews and it's simply a theory instead of historical fact.

Hmm...really Mr Barnes?

Well, let's take a look at the evidence and explore whether Hitler ordering the mass annihilation of European Jews was a mere theory, as you state, or an undeniable historical fact...

"In the summer of 1941, I cannot remember the exact date, I was suddenly summoned to the Reichsfuhrer-SS [Himmler], directly by his adjutant's office. Contrary to his usual custom, Himmler received me without his adjutant being present and said in effect: 'The Führer has ordered that the Jewish question be solved once and for all and that we, the SS, are to implement that order'."

–Rudolf Höss, excerpt from page 205 of Höss' 1959 memoir Höss, Commandant of Auschwitz

In 1922, a whole 17 years before WW2 began, Hitler told a German journalist and retired army major the following (translated by *the Nizkor Project* from journalist Major Josef Hell's *Aufzeichnung, 1922, ZS 640, p. 5, Institut fuer Zeitgeschichte*):

"Once I really am in power, my first and foremost task will be the annihilation of the Jews. As soon as I have the power to do so, I will have gallows built in rows - at the Marienplatz in Munich, for example - as many as traffic allows. Then the Jews will be hanged indiscriminately, and they will remain hanging until they stink; they will hang there as long as the principles of hygiene permit. As soon as they have been untied, the next batch will be strung up, and so on down the line, until the last Jew in Munich has been exterminated. Other cities will follow suit, precisely in this fashion, until all Germany has been completely cleansed of Jews."

The same source, incidentally, quotes Hell as saying, "His (Hitler's) eyes no longer saw me but instead bore past me and off into empty space; his explanation grew increasingly voluble until he fell into a kind of paroxysm that ended with his shouting, as if to a whole public gathering."

Years later, on January 30, 1939, Hitler left little doubt about his desire to annihilate the Jewish race from Europe in his speech to the Reichstag. An excerpt from that speech follows:

"If the international Jewish financiers in and outside Europe should succeed in plunging the nations once more into a world war, then the result will not be the Bolshevizing of the earth, and thus the victory of Jewry, but the annihilation of the Jewish race in Europe!"

That statement was proudly repeated in the 1940 Nazi propaganda film *Der ewige Jude* or, translated, *The Eternal Jew.*

"If only one country, for whatever reason, tolerates a Jewish family in it, that family will become the germ center for fresh sedition. If one little Jewish boy survives without any Jewish education, with no synagogue and no Hebrew school, it [Judaism] is in his soul. Even if there had never been a synagogue or a Jewish school or an Old Testament, the Jewish spirit would still exist and exert its influence. It has been there from the beginning and there is no Jew, not a single one, who does not personify it."

–Adolf Hitler, from a conversation with Croatian Foreign Minister General Kvaternik, July 21, 1941 (as quoted in Hitler's Apocalypse by Robert Wistrich)

"Germany's only remaining objective in the region would be limited to the annihilation of the Jews living under British protection in Arab lands."

–Adolf Hitler (in a meeting with the Mufti, Haj Amin Husseini, on 28 November 1941, as recorded in note form by Dr. Paul Otto Schmidt and quoted in pages 101-104 of Hitler and the Final Solution *by Gerald Fleming).*

Above: *Adolf Hitler, 1932.*
By Bundesarchiv, Bild
Unknown Heinrich Hoffmann
CC-BY-SA 3.0, CC BY-SA 3.0 de
Licensed under Public Domain via Wikimedia Commons

Above: *Hitler with fascist ally Benito Mussolini.*
By Muzej Revolucije Narodnosti Jugoslavije
Courtesy of United States Holocaust Memorial Museum
USHMM Photograph #89908
Licensed under Public Domain via Wikimedia Commons

FIVE

THE "HISTORY IS WRITTEN BY THE WINNERS" ARGEMENT

On September 17, 2015, USA Today Network's *The Star Press* reported on 'A Voice Among the Silent: The Legacy of James Grover McDonald,' a new documentary film that confirms it was almost common knowledge in pre-war Germany that Hitler planned to commit genocide.

The report reads, "We've all heard plenty about U.S. government officials who turned a blind eye during the Holocaust. But this month, Indiana residents are going to hear the little-known story of one of their own, an American diplomat who did everything he could to warn the world about Hitler, and help rescue European Jewish refugees."

The article mentions how McDonald was a Catholic from the Midwest with no former interest in Jewish matters. But that all changed when "during a visit to Germany in 1933, he unexpectedly found himself in private conversation with the new chancellor Adolf Hitler — and became the first American to hear the Fuhrer explicitly vow to 'get rid of the Jews'."

McDonald then began a mission to meet and warn world leaders of Hitler's agenda. Those leaders included President Franklin D. Roosevelt and Cardinal Eugenio Marìa Giuseppe Giovanni Pacelli, the future Pope Pius XII. Unfortunately, McDonald's warnings fell on deaf ears.

The Star Press report continues, "He ran into similar obstacles during his two years (1933-1935) as the League of Nations High Commissioner for Refugees Coming from Germany. During that early phase of the Nazi regime, Hitler was willing to let the Jews leave. The problem, as McDonald discovered, was that no other country was willing to receive them. He resigned as commissioner in 1935 as a protest against the failure of the international community to open its doors.

"Nonetheless, McDonald refused to be deterred. In 1938, he became chairman of the President's Advisory Committee on Political Refugees. Although its hands were largely tied by the Roosevelt administration's harsh immigration policy, McDonald and his colleagues did manage to help bring more than 2,000 Jewish refugees to the United States on the eve of the Holocaust."

What's interesting about McDonald's story is it remained unknown to most historians until 2003 when the discovery of missing pages from his diaries revealed exactly what Hitler told him.

As other (previously lost) eyewitness accounts verifying Hitler's and the Nazis' detailed plans to annihilate the Jewish people are recovered by historians each passing decade, Holocaust deniers' attempts to defend the Third Reich against accusations of genocide become more and more feeble. No, make that more and more laughable.

"These mass murders are solely the result of the Führer's policy."

–Adolf Eichmann's final speech to the court after being sentenced to death (as quoted on page 152 of Holocaust denier Paul Rassinier's book The Real Eichmann Trial).

Above: *Adolf Eichmann – one of the main organizers of the Holocaust.*

Licensed under Public Domain via Wikimedia Commons

Bundesarchiv, Bild 101I-808-1238-05
Foto: o.Ang. [4. Mai 1941]

Above: *Hitler speaks in the German parliament in 1941.*
By Bundesarchiv, Bild 101I-808-1238-05
CC-BY-SA 3.0, CC BY-SA 3.0 de
Licensed under Public Domain via Wikimedia Commons

"The discovery of the Jewish virus is one of the greatest revolutions that has taken place in the world. The battle in which we are engaged today is of the same sort as the battle waged, during the last century, by Pasteur and Koch. How many diseases have their origin in the Jewish virus! ... We shall regain our health only by eliminating the Jew."

–Adolf Hitler (quoted in The Racial State: Germany 1933-1945 *by Michael Burleigh and Wolfgang Wippermann)*

Regarding *Mein Kampf,* we'd have to agree with the reviewer who said, "Mein Kampf is a terribly written book. It is incoherent and full of random ramblings. It's over 600 pages long and in dire need of a good editor."

One of the most insightful reviews of *Mein Kampf* we could find appears on the *WhistlingInTheWind.org* site. In answer to the question "Why would I want to read a book by one of the most evil men in history?" the reviewer says, "Hitler was unlike anyone else. His vicious hatred and the horrific acts he committed are something that none of us can understand. So out of historical curiosity, I decided to try and get an insight into the mind of this dictator (to see) how could he possibly justify his evil ideology."

Excerpts from the review follow:

"Historians have gone through it and found that most of what he claims is false and he leaves out huge parts of his life... The most common theme in the book is how much Hitler hates the Jews...(and) what was surprising was how blatant Hitler was in his hatred. Literally every discussion ended with Hitler blaming the Jews. He almost always referred to Jews in the singular as though there was only one type and they all acted the same way...

"Anti-Semitism isn't just one of Hitler's views; it's his main one on which he bases the rest of his views. Mein Kampf is therefore bursting with the worst possible form of insults and hatred for the Jews. They are frequently called vermin and parasites and never described in human terms. The Jews were 'a pestilence, a moral pestilence with which the public was being infected. It was worse than the Black Plague of long ago'. Always sub human terms and no insult was too much. Hitler encouraged hatred of the Jews and expected people to go out of their way to antagonise the Jews...

"There were some truly bizarre/disturbing/crazy passages when Hitler went full crazy in his paranoia and hatred of the Jews...He literally believed the world was divided into different races with some superior and other inferior. He placed a high priority on keeping the German race 'pure' of 'contamination'."

Most subscribers (to *Whistling In The Wind*) praise the review. Most, but not all. One or two, who obviously have their own agendas, attempt to downplay Hitler's emphasis on the Jews. One even blames the translation (from German to English) for certain facts being misconstrued or lost in translation.

It's funny how some people attempt to defend the indefensible, isn't it?

"Today I had a very long talk about the Jews with Himmler. I said that the world would no longer tolerate the extermination of the Jews; it was high time that he put a stop to it. Himmler said that it was beyond his power; he was not the Führer and Adolf Hitler had expressly ordered it. I asked him whether he was aware that history would one day point to him as one of the greatest murderers on record, because of the way in which he had exterminated the Jews. He should think of his reputation, not sully it with that reproach. Himmler replied that he had done nothing wrong and only carried out Adolf Hitler's orders. ... I told Himmler that he still had a chance to stand well with history by showing humanity to the Jews and other victims of the concentration camp -- if he really disagreed with Hitler's orders to exterminate them. He could simply forget certain of the Führer's orders and not carry them out ... "Perhaps you're right, Herr Kersten," Himmler responded, but he also added that the Führer would never forgive him and would immediately have him hanged."

–Felix Kersten (Heinrich Himmler's personal manual therapist), The Kersten Memoirs

Above: *Heinrich Himmler shaking hands with the Führer.*
By Bundesarchiv, Bild 183-H28988 / Hoffmann /
CC-BY-SA 3.0, CC BY-SA 3.0 de
https://commons.wikimedia.org/w/index.php?curid=9070280
Licensed under Public Domain via Wikimedia Commons

SIX

MYTH #5: "The reason the real story about the Holocaust cannot ever be proven, or disproven, is because it is taboo. If you publicly want to discuss the numbers, depending on what country you are in, you may be arrested. Why? If the Holocaust is so well documented then why not just prove it to shut up the deniers? Why forbid deniers from presenting their version of history?"

—Anonymous Holocaust denier #5

It's not remotely a taboo to investigate the Holocaust. Even in Europe, where there are strict laws in place outlawing denial of crimes against humanity – and thereby outlawing denial of the Holocaust – you can study historical records of the Holocaust and inspect Nazi documentation relating to it until your heart's content. You will even be encouraged to do this.

Such laws, incidentally, are in place in a number of European countries, including Germany, Austria, Poland, France and Romania, and they were primarily introduced in the 1990s to combat the alarming rise of white supremacists and neo-Nazis. Only in Romania do the laws exclusively relate to the Holocaust, and only in Israel, where similar laws are in place, are Jews specifically mentioned.

Although these anti-denial laws have been criticized by some freedom-of-speech proponents, they serve as a permanent and useful reminder that the Holocaust was the worst crime in living memory, and that there are very real concerns that history could repeat itself.

However, laws outlawing denial of crimes against humanity (and thereby the Holocaust) do not – repeat *do not* – equate to a cover-up of (the real history of) the Holocaust. The real history – i.e. the proof – is there for all to see...in plain sight.

And as for those freedom-of-speech concerns, it is admittedly a rather drastic measure to make any opinion of history, however silly or dangerous, illegal, and it has even divided Holocaust survivors and those who fight to keep the memory of the Holocaust alive. Some say that freedom of speech is among the rights that the free world fought to maintain in their struggle against the fascists. For example, in a 2006 *BBC* online news article headlined "Holocaust denier Irving is jailed," which mentioned that David Irving was "found guilty in Vienna of denying the Holocaust of European Jewry and sentenced to three years in prison," it was also reported that Irving's old foe Deborah E. Lipstadt said, "I am not happy when censorship wins, and I don't believe in winning battles via censorship...The way of fighting Holocaust deniers is with history and with truth."

On the other hand, there are many others who believe that if some anti-Semitic, Nazi-sympathizing,

Holocaust-denying, Hitler apologist publically states the Holocaust has been greatly exaggerated, or, worse, never happened, he or she deserves to be prosecuted to the letter of the law. In other words, they should have the book thrown at them or else they should be whacked over the head with a hardback copy of *Mein Kampf* until they see sense!

Whichever side of the fence you stand on this issue, perhaps it is not that drastic or unusual when you consider there are laws against denial of specific genocides besides the Holocaust in other countries.

For example, it is against the law to deny the Holodomor in the Ukraine. "After independence in 1991," a 2013 *EuroNews* article states, "a law in Ukraine made it a criminal offence to deny that the Holodomor was pre-meditated genocide."

In various other nations there are specific laws in place against Armenian Genocide denial, Bosnian Genocide denial, Rwandan Genocide denial and Serbian Genocide denial, to name but a few. So the theory that Jews are somehow orchestrating all these laws (and in countries they barely reside in anymore), is ill-researched to say the least.

Even in America there are limits of expression.

Ask yourself this: If we, as (non-American) authors, embarked on a speaking tour around the US aimed at convincing Americans that the ancestors of African-Americans were never slaves, millions never died in the slave trade and that claims to the contrary are simply propaganda, do you think US authorities would not cancel the tour or revoke our visitor visas? Notwithstanding the *First Amendment* and America's rather liberal freedom of speech laws, the potential for violence arising from our tour would surely result in the tour being stopped and, most likely, our deportation. Fair enough, too.

And the potential for such violent racial crimes arising from Holocaust denial is arguably even higher in Europe and the Middle East given anti-Semitism is increasing, not decreasing.

"Both incest and the Holocaust have been subject to furious denial by perpetrators and other individuals and by highly organized groups such as the False Memory Syndrome Foundation and the Committee for Historical Review. Incest and the Holocaust are vulnerable to this kind of concerted denial because of their unfathomability, the unjustifiability, and the threat they pose to the politics of patriarchy and anti-Semitism respectively. Over and over, survivors of the Holocaust attest that they were warned of what was happening in Poland but could not believe it at the time, could not believe it later as it was happening to them, and still to this day cannot believe what they, at the same time, know to have occurred. For Holocaust deniers this is a felicitous twist, for their arguments denying the Holocaust ... capitalize on the discrepancies of faded memory. In the case of incest, although post-traumatic stress disorder, amnesia, and dissociation represent some of the mind's strategies for comprehending the incomprehensible, incest deniers have taken advantage of inconsistencies to discredit survivor testimony."

–Janet Walker, *Trauma Cinema: Documenting Incest and the Holocaust*

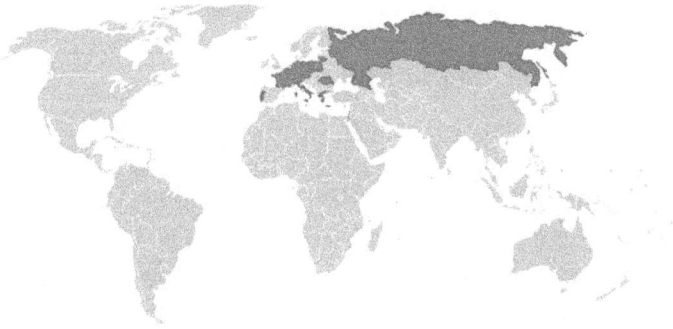

Above: *Countries (in red) where Holocaust denial is prohibited by law.*

By Dima st bk - Holocaustdenial.gif, CC BY-SA 4.0

Licensed under Public Domain via Wikimedia Commons

As mentioned, laws against crimes against humanity (not just the Holocaust) were primarily introduced to defend against the new wave of white supremacists and neo-Nazis.

There is no doubt anti-Semitism is rearing its ugly head once more. Try Googling "incidents of anti-Semitism" or scanning the headlines of major metropolitan newspapers if you don't believe this.

Here's a headline in *The Atlantic*, dated February 17, 2015 that caught our eye. It reads, "Europe's Increasingly Targeted Jews Take Stock." The sub-heading is even more alarming. It reads, "Old fears are stoked as anti-Semitic attacks increase."

Atlantic staff writer Conor Friedersdorf states, "After recent anti-Semitic murders in Paris and Copenhagen, Israeli Prime Minister Benjamin Netanyahu called on European Jews to leave the continent. He urged them to go to Israel, 'your home.' Of course, their home is France or Denmark or whatever their country of residence. But as Zack Beauchamp notes, outside of the United States, attacks on Jews have been rising over the last decade, and many are now wondering if Europe will remain their home forever.

"Politicians are wondering too. 'Prime Minister Manuel Valls has urged France's Jews not to emigrate after the desecration of some 300 Jewish graves,' BBC News reported Monday in another appalling story of apparent anti-Semitism in France. A day earlier, Israeli journalist Zvika Klein published an even more depressing piece after donning a yarmulke and walking around Paris for a day with a hidden camera."

Friedersdorf quotes Klein as saying, "Areas known as tourist attractions were relatively calm, but the further from them we walked, the more anxious I became over the hateful stares, the belligerent remarks, and the hostile body language... In one of the mostly-Muslim neighborhoods... I was lambasted with expletives."

Friedersdorf continues, "The moments captured on the video would be disgusting even as anomalies, and the statistics about anti-Semitic attacks in France suggest they're only getting more common.

"Last year, an essay by Michel Gurfinkiel, 'You Only Live Twice,' argued that Jews experienced a Golden Age in Western Europe during the years after World War II, but that 'since 2000, (some) 7,650 anti-Semitic incidents have been reliably reported to...the French ministry of the interior; this figure omits incidents known to have occurred but unreported to the police. The incidents range from hate speech, anti-Semitic graffiti, and verbal threats to defacement of synagogues and other Jewish buildings, to acts of violence and terror including arson, bombings, and murder."

On January 12, 2015, the *Mail Online* reports "Jews are fleeing terror-hit Paris because of growing anti-Semitism in France, one of Britain's most influential Jewish journalists said today."

The article continues, "Stephen Pollard, editor of the Jewish Chronicle, spoke out after an Islamic terrorist took six people hostage and held them captive in a Kosher supermarket in the French capital.

"This afternoon police ordered all shops in a famous Jewish neighborhood in central Paris to close.

"The mayor's office in Paris announced the closure of shops along the Rosiers street in Paris' Marais neighborhood, in the heart of the tourist district and less than a mile away from the offices of satirical magazine Charlie Hebdo where 12 people were killed on Wednesday.

"Hours before the Jewish Sabbath, the street is usually crowded with French Jews and tourists alike.

"Mr Pollard said today's terror attack in Paris, linked to the massacre at the office of Charlie Hebdo, will force more French Jews to flee the country.

"Many are moving to Britain or to Israel, according to a report published in the newspaper last year.

"He said the fact that a terrorist had chosen to target a Jewish store was no 'fluke'.

"In a series of tweets he said: 'Every single French Jew I know has either left or is actively working out how to leave'... 'What's going on in France - outrages that have been getting worse for years - put our antisemitism problems in perspective'.

"The hostage situation in the Porte de Vincennes part of the city is ongoing today...18 months ago France had around 500,000 Jewish residents - the largest population in the EU - but experts expect the number to fall to 400,000 within a few years, Mr Pollard's newspaper said."

The aforementioned essay titled "You Only Live Twice," by Michel Gurfinkiel, founder and president of the Jean-Jacques Rousseau Institute, a conservative think-tank in France, paints an even more dismal picture for Jews living in modern-day Europe.

Published on August 5, 2013, in *Mosaic*, a magazine dedicated to "Advancing Jewish thought," the article reads in part as follows:

Above: Anti-Semitic graffiti in Lithuania (2005).

By Beny Shlevich

http://flickr.com/photos/shlevich/37431682/,
CC BY-SA 2.0

Licensed under Public Domain via Wikimedia Commons

"The Paradox (is that) European Judaism looks healthy, and secure. Religious and cultural activities are everywhere on the rise... In Paris, a European Center for Judaism will soon be built under the auspices of the Consistoire (the French union of synagogues) and the French government. Many European capitals now harbor major Jewish museums or Holocaust memorials...

"And yet, despite all their success and achievement, the majority of European Jews, seconded by many Jewish and non-Jewish experts, insist that catastrophe may lie ahead.

"One does not have to look far to see why. A large-scale survey commissioned by the European Union's Agency for Fundamental Rights (FRA) tells a tale of widespread and persistent anti-Semitism...

"Among the findings: more than one in four Jews report experiencing anti-Semitic harassment at least once in the twelve months preceding the survey; one in three have experienced such harassment over the past five years; just under one in ten have experienced a physical attack or threat in the same period; and between two-fifths and one-half in France, Belgium, and Hungary have considered emigrating because they feel unsafe... All over Europe, with exceptions here and there, the story is much the same...

"For many European Jews, there is indeed a déjà vu quality to the present situation. Like Israelis, but unlike most American Jews, today's European Jews are survivors, or children of survivors, either of the Holocaust or of the near-complete expulsion of Jews from Islamic countries that took place in the second half of the 20th century. They know, from personal experience or from the testimony of direct and irrefutable witnesses, how things unfolded in the not too distant past, and how a seemingly normal Jewish life could be destroyed overnight."

Gurfinkiel concludes, "When anti-Semitic incidents or other problems accumulate, they can't help asking whether history is repeating itself."

Anti-Semitism is on the rise in Britain, too. Commenting on a *Daily Mail* article published on December 17, 2015, *The Jerusalem Post* reports, "Anti-Semitic, anti-Muslim hate crimes rise significantly in London."

The article reads, "The number of anti-Semitic and anti-Muslim hate crimes recorded this year by police in London was 61 percent higher than in 2014.

"The figures released this week by the Metropolitan Police listed 483 anti-Semitic hate crimes documented over the 12 months that preceded Nov. 1, 2015. In the previous 12-month stretch, 299 incidents were reported...

"Commenting on the statistics, a spokesperson for the Community Security Trust, or CST, which is British Jewry's watchdog and security service, told the Jewish News of London: "Any rise in anti-Semitic hate crimes is of concern. We hope that this reflects improved confidence amongst victims and witnesses to report hate crimes to the police as well as any rise in the number of hate crimes taking place."

Given the rise in anti-Semitism – around the world, but especially in Europe – it would seem those strict laws in place outlawing denial of crimes against humanity in various European countries are doing little to address racist attitudes toward the Jewish community.

Deniers, of course, have targeted these laws, claiming the regulations are all part of a Jewish mega-conspiracy to inflate the number of Holocaust victims.

One such denier to use these laws as a sly way of implying there is a cover-up of the truth on Holocaust history is former president of Iran, Mahmoud Ahmadinejad, who delivered a speech on September 18, 2009, which aired on IRINN, stating: "Of course, some governments and their people always hated the Jews because of the ugly conduct of some of them... If the Holocaust that you talk about was real, why don't you allow the subject to be studied? One can freely research any issue, except for this issue, which is sealed. It is a black box, which they do not allow to be opened or reexamined. They do this in order to exploit it."

Ahmadinejad and other deniers conveniently overlook the fact that the laws were introduced long after the Holocaust and that for around forty to fifty years anyone was openly allowed to deny the historicity of the Holocaust anywhere, and many did!

And those who claim the laws have been influenced by Jewish lobby groups should keep in mind the laws do *not* apply to the likes of the US, Britain or Russia – countries which all have large numbers of Jewish citizens – where denial of the Holocaust *is* legal. Nor do they stop to consider it is *illegal* in countries like Lithuania and Romania where there are now few Jews to be found.

Above: Former President of Iran, Mahmoud Ahmadinejad.

Widely reported as an anti-Semite and a Holocaust denier.

By Foto: Marcello Casal Jr\ABr -
http://www.agenciabrasil.gov.br/media/imagens/2009/11/23/23110
9MCA0340.jpg/view

(now at: http://memoria.ebc.com.br/agenciabrasil/galeria/2009-11-
22/23-de-novembro-de-2009 / .jpg),

CC BY 3.0 br

Licensed under Public Domain via Wikimedia Commons

"The nationalist not only does not disapprove of atrocities committed by his own side, but he has a remarkable capacity for not even hearing about them. For quite six years the English admirers of Hitler contrived not to learn of the existence of Dachau and Buchenwald. And those who are loudest in denouncing the German concentration camps are often quite unaware, or only very dimly aware, that there are also concentration camps in Russia. Huge events like the Ukraine famine of 1933, involving the deaths of millions of people, have actually escaped the attention of the majority of English russophiles. Many English people have heard almost nothing about the extermination of German and Polish Jews during the present war. Their own antisemitism has caused this vast crime to bounce off their consciousness. In nationalist thought there are facts which are both true and untrue, known and unknown. A known fact may be so unbearable that it is habitually pushed aside and not allowed to enter into logical processes, or on the other hand it may enter into every calculation and yet never be admitted as a fact, even in one's own mind."

–George Orwell, Notes on Nationalism

To our knowledge, Israel is the only country in the world that has specifically criminalized denial of the Holocaust itself. Israel also specifically mentions Jews in these laws, alluding to most Holocaust denial stemming from anti-Semitic beliefs.

The Jerusalem Post, July 20, 2004 reports, "Legislation that would make Holocaust-denial committed overseas an offense under Israeli legal jurisdiction was approved unanimously in first reading by the Knesset on Tuesday...The passage of the measure would enable Israel to demand the extradition of Holocaust-deniers for prosecution."

The article continues, "The bill was drafted...as a move against former Palestinian Authority prime minister Mahmoud Abbas (Abu Mazen) for his doctoral dissertation 20 years ago in which he estimated that the Nazis killed less than a million Jews.

"It is likely to serve as a deterrence [sic. deterrent] against Holocaust-deniers visiting Israel, although the possibility of countries consenting to extradition on the offense is unlikely.

"The legislation expands the territorial jurisdiction of the Israeli law against Holocaust-denying outside of it [sic] borders."

The same article appears on the Rense Radio Network conspiracy theory site *Rense.com* – and it seems not all subscribers (to the network's site) approve of the Knesset's actions. This vitriolic response (unabridged) was posted by one subscriber:

"Who do these arrogant bastards think they are? The audacity to think that a group of Jews can control the thoughts and ideas of others outside of their own nation?! To attempt control them, silence them, hold power and sway --- ah! --- can anyone read this report without seeing the obvious? When someone says these people are too small and insignificant in the world to be part of some evil cartel seeking world domination... doesn't something like this just flash a bright light in ones eyes and wake you up to what is apparent?! It doesn't take a rocket scientist to see that they seek the power over the very minds of everyone else on earth and want to bring them into their own jurisdiction and meet out punishment for just the suggestion, just the mere thought that Holocaust numbers might be exaggerated or inaccurate. Anyone who can read this and not see the sickening arrogance of the Zionists in Israel has a screw loose."

We think this particular Rense subscriber and others of his ilk would benefit from studying history beyond the obscure conspiracy theory books and other anti-Semitic literature they no doubt read.

"Denial is the eighth stage that always follows a genocide. It is among the surest indicators of further genocidal massacres. The perpetrators of genocide dig up the mass graves, burn the bodies, try to cover up the evidence and intimidate the witnesses. They deny that they committed any crimes, and often blame what happened on the victims."

—Gregory H. Stanton, formerly of the US State Department and the founder of Genocide Watch, from the article The 8 Stages of Genocide.

As a footnote on these laws against Holocaust denial, there is a strange twist occurring in Poland on the eve of this book's publication.

A March 22, 2016 article written by Vanessa Gera, of the *Associated Press*, describes how the new government of Poland is attempting to silence Holocaust debates. But not in the way you'd imagine.

"Poland's governing party is seeking to shape the country's future by controlling perceptions of the past," Gera writes.

The conservative Law and Justice Party are, according to the article, attempting "to suppress discussion and research into painful topics, primarily Polish violence against Jews during the Nazi occupation."

Gera continues, "Law and Justice, which since last year has wielded more power than any party in post-communist times, sees the moves as harnessing history in a mission to build a stronger nation state. President Andrzej Duda said the nation's new 'historical policy offensive' aims to create a new generation of patriots and 'to build up the country's position in the international space'."

Critics view Poland's new measures as historical revisionism. They point out that while highlighting the very real fact that millions of Poles died at the hands of the Nazis, one aim is to bury the massive number of incidents where Poles murdered and betrayed defenseless Jews.

The article quotes Pawel Spiewak, director of the Jewish Historical Institute, in Warsaw, as saying, "They want to narrow our view of the past. They want to use the state apparatus to force their new view of political history, and this is very dangerous."

Spiewak also expressed fear that under the new laws employees at the Jewish Historical Institute, some of whom include Holocaust survivors, may be imprisoned for retelling exactly what occurred in Poland before and during WW2.

Incidentally, Polish President Duda sparked international outrage in early 2016 when his office announced it is considering stripping Poland-born American and Princeton Holocaust scholar, Jan

Tomasz Gross, of a national Polish honor he received in 1996.

Historian Jan Grabowski, author of *Hunt for the Jews: Betrayal and Murder in German-Occupied Poland*, stated that Duda's approach "is a huge step backwards from the historical truth and towards a more aggressive abuse of the memory of the Holocaust."

To quote Vanessa Gera, of the *Associated Press*, again, she writes, "The historical offensive comes amid a strong anti-migrant mood in Poland and as the ruling party is also centralizing its power in a way that undermines democratic institutions, most dramatically the independence of the constitutional court.

"The trend resembles recent moves in Hungary, where historical revisionism has gone hand-in-hand with Prime Minister Viktor Orban's creation of what he calls an 'illiberal state.' Hungarian authorities have been rehabilitating wartime anti-Semites and portraying the country as the victim of German aggression when it in fact was allied with Hitler most of the war."

Gera concludes by stating, "The high emotions surrounding Polish wartime behavior touch on what some call a Polish 'obsession with innocence' — a conviction the nation is morally blameless thanks to its resistance and widespread suffering, with millions killed in the war."

Could it be that the political leaders of Poland and several other EU countries *still* have not learned the lessons of the past and even continue to silently harbor anti-Semitic beliefs?

*"There is a psychological dimension to the
deniers' and minimizers' objectives: The
general public tends to accord victims of
genocide a certain moral authority. If you
devictimize a people you strip them of their
moral authority, and if you can in turn claim to
be a victim, as the Poles and Austrians often try
to do, that moral authority is conferred on or
restored to you."*

–*Deborah E. Lipstadt,* Denying the Holocaust: The
Growing Assault on Truth and Memory

Above: *Corpse of a starved Jewish infant.
Warsaw Ghetto, Poland, 1942.
Jewish cemetery in Okopowa Street, Warsaw.
By Unknown - Emil Apfelbaum (1946) Choroba głodowa.
Licensed under Public Domain via Wikimedia Commons*

SEVEN

MYTH #6: "Why is it so hard to believe that history can be altered or even completely fictionalized by those who control the world's money supply and own massive propaganda machines like Hollywood? I mean, you cannot deny that Jews have a huge influence in the banking/financial world and in the media, can you?"

—*Anonymous Holocaust denier #6*

No, we wouldn't deny Jews are very influential in the financial sector and in the media.

But we would go much further than that.

Jews have made an enormous mark in virtually every field known to man: from mathematics to publishing, from science to psychiatry, music, medicine, economics, human rights campaigning and engineering – and quite a few more besides.

When you consider there are only about 13 million Jews worldwide (about half of the population of

Mexico City) they are undeniably an incredible people. To call them high achievers is an understatement. And it's not just in the modern era that they greatly influenced all the aforementioned disparate, intellectual spheres; they've been enormously influential since Ancient times.

Professor Huston Smith, whom we should point out is a gentile (non-Jew), effectively summarizes the history of the global influence of Jewish people in his book *The Religions of Man*. In it, Smith writes, "There is a striking point that runs through Jewish history as a whole. Western civilization was born in the Middle East, and the Jews were at its crossroads. In the heyday of Rome, the Jews were close to the Empire's center. When power shifted eastward, the Jewish center was in Babylon; when it skipped to Spain, there again were the Jews. When in the Middle Ages the center of civilization moved into Central Europe, the Jews were waiting for it in Germany and Poland. The rise of the United States to the leading world power found Judaism focused there. And now, today, when the pendulum seems to be swinging back toward the Old World and the East rises to renewed importance, there again are the Jews in Israel."

All that despite never having a country of their own until the mid-20th Century; *and* despite being up against a veritable avalanche of anti-Semitism in every other country they have resided in; *and* all too often not being allowed to attend certain learning institutions or permitted to work in certain fields because of who they were and their religion.

Throughout history, the Jews have largely sculpted the world many of us live in. Certainly here in the West that's true.

Do the research and you will find, as we did, that Jews were, and often still are, at the forefront of many important international movements, including women's rights, the legal equality of races, child welfare, animal rights and environmental protection. It's difficult to fathom how many of these initiatives would have progressed as far as they have, or in some cases even gotten off the ground when they did, without Jewish input.

Another gentile, English historian Paul Johnson, highlights the irrefutable Jewish influence on our evolving civilization in his book, *A History of the Jews.*

Johnson writes, "Certainly, the world without the Jews would have been a radically different place. Humanity might have eventually stumbled upon all the Jewish insights. But we cannot be sure. All the great conceptual discoveries of the human intellect seem obvious and inescapable once they had been revealed, but it requires a special genius to formulate them for the first time. The Jews had this gift. To them we owe the idea of equality before the law, both divine and human; of the sanctity of life and the dignity of human person; of the individual conscience and so a personal redemption; of collective conscience and so of social responsibility; of peace as an abstract ideal and love as the foundation of justice, and many other items which constitute the basic moral furniture of the human mind. Without Jews it might have been a much emptier place."

It is perhaps no coincidence that many Nobel Prize winners have been Jewish. At least 25% (yes one quarter) of all Nobel laureates have been Jewish – a disproportionality high ratio considering only 0.2% of the world's population is Jewish. (For nonmathematicians like ourselves that equates to considerably less than 1% of humanity).

Such a mind-blowing statistic is enough to perplex even the brightest minds. Take, for example, the normally vociferous bestselling author, biologist and atheist Richard Dawkins. He states in a 2013 interview with the *New Republic* that he's "intrigued by" the "phenomenally high" number of Jewish laureates.

And well over a century ago, the great American author Mark Twain also pondered the mystery of Jewish influence in his essay "Concerning The Jews," which was published in an 1899 edition of *Harper's Magazine*.

In that essay, Twain writes, "If the statistics are right, the Jews constitute but one percent of the human race. It suggests a nebulous dim puff of stardust lost in the blaze of the Milky way. ... The Jew ought hardly to be heard of, but he is heard of, has always been heard of. He is as prominent on the planet as any other people, and his commercial importance is extravagantly out of proportion to the smallness of his bulk. His contributions to the world's list of great names in literature, science, art, music, finance, medicine, and abstruse learning are also away out of proportion to the weakness of his numbers. He has made a marvelous fight in this world, in all the ages; and had done it with his hands tied behind him. He could be vain of himself, and be excused for it."

The Russian master of literature Leo Tolstoy also pondered the curious and unique history of these people in his essay *What is the Jew?*, as quoted in page 189 of *The Final Resolution*, a 1908 edition of *the Jewish World periodical*.

"What is the Jew?" Tolstoy asks. "What kind of unique creature is this whom all the rulers of all the nations of the world have disgraced and crushed and expelled and destroyed; persecuted, burned and drowned, and who, despite their anger and their fury, continues to live and to flourish. What is this Jew whom they have never succeeded in enticing with all the enticements in the world, whose oppressors and persecutors only suggested that he deny (and disown) his religion and cast aside the faithfulness of his ancestors?!

"The Jew – is the symbol of eternity," Tolstoy continues. "He is the one who for so long had guarded the prophetic message and transmitted it to all mankind. A people such as this can never disappear. The Jew is eternal. He is the embodiment of eternity."

"I saw a remarkable study of the five most influential people of all time: Moses, Jesus, Marx, Freud, & Einstein – all Jewish!"

–*Rabbi Wein*

We are not for a moment implying the Jews are superior to other peoples. Nor are we buying into the *Chosen People* moniker that has been bestowed upon them in the Bible as we are not even sure what that means, and we sense it may be more of a figurative, symbolic or metaphorical description than a literal one. We are simply reporting the undeniable fact that our planet would be much worse off without the Jews, and they, like all races, have something unique to offer.

Above: *Albert Einstein – one of around 200 Jewish Nobel laureates.*

Official 1921 Nobel Prize in Physics photograph

Licensed under Public Domain via Wikimedia Commons

Their culture and contribution should be celebrated, not despised, downgraded or ignored.

We are also highlighting the Jews' achievements and their service to humanity because we believe their success has a lot to do with the hatred and persecution they've received in the past and continue to receive to this day.

It is very evident many non-Jews simply cannot believe that so small a minority can achieve so much in virtually every field without their being scoundrels or corrupt. Furthermore, many anti-Semites would have us believe Jews are all part of some uber-conspiracy that allows them to craftily rise without merit to the top of their chosen fields.

Can you imagine if, say, half the world's most successful people came from the West African nation of Senegal? (Senegal's population is roughly the equivalent of the global Jewish population). So, following this analogy through, it wouldn't be long before jealousy reared its ugly head and people would say things like, "Those Senegalese are liars and cheats and are secretly controlling the world!"

Setting aside the fundamentalist, Far Right and extremist versions of Christianity and Islam, where anti-Semitism thrives, it is plainly obvious to us that the success of these brilliant and community-orientated people is one of the main reasons the Jews have been envied and harassed down through history – and is partly why the Nazis wanted to annihilate them.

It's also worth noting the overwhelming statistics verifying the phenomenon of disproportionate Jewish success is something of a taboo subject in virtually all circles; anti-Semites do not want to admit to *any* legitimate or well-earned achievements of their perceived enemies; Jewish people themselves do not generally want to discuss their community's successes in public for fear of being labeled big-headed – or worse, being accused of promoting Jewish superiority myths; academics also usually avoid the topic, possibly out of fear of inadvertently entering into racial debates.

We, however, as impartial observers with no allegiance to any sides (whether those sides be Jews, gentiles or academics), feel it is too important a topic to omit in a book assessing the reasons for anti-Semitism, which all too often spirals into Holocaust denial.

Rabbi Levi Brackman is one of the few Jews we have come across who is comfortable discussing and writing about the subject. In a 2008 article published on *Ynet News*, Rabbi Brackman writes that, "The fact that Jews are disproportionally successful in many fields of endeavor is undeniable. The statistics simply speak for themselves. Jews make up less than half of one percent of the world's population but they consistently have made up more than twenty percent of the Forbes 400 list of the world richest people.

"But it is not just making money that a disproportionate amount of Jews seems to excel at. Thirty percent of Nobel Prize winners in science are Jewish. ... In virtually every industry successful Jews are disproportionally represented."

As you would expect of a rabbi, Brackman goes on to state his belief that the religion of Judaism is at least partially responsible for disproportionate success of his people. However, he also admits that the statistics surrounding Jewish influence remains a mystery and notes that "others surmise that it is related to our intense persecution."

That final point may have some truth to it. As the Rabbi alludes, of the few scholars who have written about this subject some have suggested that because Jews have been persecuted throughout history it has forced them, generation after generation, to be more creative. Essentially, this theory proposes that to survive centuries of oppression the worldwide Jewish community needed to become as educated as possible, work harder than the average person to achieve the same results and never rest on their laurels. Some have even theorized this fight for survival caused certain positive changes in the Jewish DNA during the last few thousand years of evolution.

We don't claim that's the answer to this mystery, nor do we profess to have any ideas to help solve it, but there's one thing we do know for sure: the supposedly mutually exclusive subjects of Jewish influence and accomplishments, the *real* history of the Jews and the enduring conspiracy theory that they control the world are in reality all inexorably related to each other – not to mention all being crucial to understanding Holocaust denial.

So for the rest of this chapter, we shall now attempt to reveal the subtle or somewhat hidden connections between all these complex subjects...

Above: A small selection of prominent Jews from past &
present, including Maccabeus, Josephus, Freud, Einstein,
Natalie Portman.

By Various (See source images for details) –

Judas Maccabeus Josephus Akiva ben Joseph Maimonides

Baruch Spinoza Sigmund Freud Sholem Aleichem

Albert Einstein Emmy Noether David Ben-Gurion

Marc Chagall Natalie Portman, CC BY-SA 3.0,

Licensed under Public Domain via Wikimedia Commons

> *"Anti-semitism is a form of underdog resentment and envy, directed at another underdog who has made it in American society. The remarkable upward mobility of American Jews--rooted chiefly in a history and culture that places a premium on higher education and self-organization--easily lends itself to myths of Jewish unity and homogeneity that have gained currency among other groups, especially among relatively unorganized groups like black Americans. The high visibility of Jews in the upper reaches of the academy, journalism, the entertainment industry, and the professions--though less so percentage-wise in corporate America and national political office--is viewed less as a result of hard work and success fairly won and more as a matter of favoritism and nepotism among Jews."*

–*Cornel West*, Race Matters

The banking field is an area we can comment with some authority on, having co-authored a non-fiction book on international bankers and high finance. So we can confirm there are many leading Jewish bankers, but remember there are leading Jewish figures in almost every field, so it means very little in the grand scheme of things.

The elite banking dynasty of Rothschilds, whose family members are indeed Jewish, are just one of dozens of major banking dynasties worldwide. Some are Jewish, many are non-Jewish.

The Rothschilds are people we certainly would not attempt to defend given the rumors swirling around them of financial corruption and market manipulation in this era and in earlier eras. However, the way they are held up, by conspiracy extremists and other paranoid thinkers, to represent the Jewish community is an absolute joke. There are good and bad people in all races. The fact that there are many Jews in the banking sector is being used by neo-Nazis and anti-Semites to try to sway the uneducated to believe the Jews are the problem instead of banking shysters and banksters in general.

Another important point relating to the current Jewish prominence in the banking world is there is a very obvious historical reason for it.

As we alluded to earlier, historically Jews did not have much freedom of choice when it came to their occupations. In fact, they were once forbidden by Christian authorities, and by some Muslim authorities, to pursue most regular occupations. They were, however, permitted and even encouraged to enter the banking industry because, in the medieval era at least, Christians/Muslims were not allowed to charge fellow-Christians/Muslims interest, but *someone* had to make loans – so the Jews were charged with the task.

Jews were also permitted to slaughter animals – another equally unsavory job – and they were then despised and mocked by entire communities for being animal slaughterers and bankers.

A November 2014 article by Gergory Myers on the *KnowledgeNuts* site confirms this little-known history of the beginnings of the banking industry.

The article, titled 'Jewish People Were Forced To Become Moneylenders', begins by outlining the basic myth: "The conspiracies about Jewish bankers go back a long way and are so ingrained that even many people who are not anti-Semitic buy into the theory. Historically, there have been many Jewish people involved in banking, but it was never a conspiracy. In actuality, due to usury laws prescribed by the Jewish scriptures, the Jewish people were considered the logical choice to handle the moneylending. To make matters worse, many Jewish people were barred from other occupations, so they had to take what they could get."

Myers continues, "Many people still claim that there is an international banking conspiracy run by a shadowy group of Jewish men who control . . . literally everything in the world. Now, it is true that there are a lot of big Jewish family names in banking and that many of them go back a very long way. But there is no conspiracy. The Jewish people never planned to take over anything or become the banking force that many of them still are today. In fact, when they first started to transform into the forerunners of the modern bankers we see today, they basically had no other choice when it came to a profession.

"They existed to perform an important role but were often given as few rights as possible. To make matters worse, they were used as scapegoats by the government so people would be angry at the Jewish people for moneylending practices, instead of being angry at their government for high taxes and poor standards of living."

The concept of Jews being scapegoats resonates to this very day as scaremongers, paranoid thinkers and (some) conspiracy theorists base their beliefs on unfounded rumors and gossip rather than the facts. Facts that are staring them in the face if they only care to look.

Sadly, it seems nothing much has changed after centuries of anti-Semitism *and* after the Holocaust.

"I wanted to tell him a story, but I didn't. It's a story about a Jew riding in a streetcar, in Germany during the Third Reich, reading Goebbels' paper, the Volkische Beobachter. A non-Jewish acquaintance sits down next to him and says, "Why do you read the Beobachter?" "Look," says the Jew, "I work in a factory all day. When I get home, my wife nags me, the children are sick, and there's no money for food. What should I do on my way home, read the Jewish newspaper? 'Pogrom in Romania,' 'Jews Murdered in Poland.' 'New Laws against Jews.' No, sir, a half-hour a day, on the streetcar, I read the Beobachter. 'Jews the World Capitalists,' 'Jews Control Russia,' 'Jews Rule in England.' That's me they're talking about. A half-hour a day I'm somebody. Leave me alone, friend."

–Milton Sanford Mayer

How does this supposed conspiracy of *the Jewish people controlling the world* relate to Holocaust denial, you may ask?

Well, believe it or not, many people are so fearful of Jewish people – whether they be Jews in Israel, the United States, the United Kingdom, Australia or wherever – they are convinced this tiny minority of 13 million people is secretly ruling the world's 7.5 billion people *and* can effortlessly revise any episode of history *and* can fake such well-documented and scientifically-proven historical events as the Holocaust.

One classic example of such paranoia was Canadian public school teacher James Keegstra (1934-2014) who was convicted of hate speech crimes in 1984. Keegstra taught his social studies students that the Holocaust was a hoax created by "evil Jews" and, besides trotting out all the usual anti-Semitic insults, even went as far as calling Jewish people "child killers."

In the 1985 book, *A Trust Betrayed: The Keegstra Affair,* by David Wertheimer and Douglas Bercuson, it was mentioned that Keegstra taught his young students that the Jews "created the Holocaust to gain sympathy" and are the antithesis of Christians in that they (the Jews) are scheming, subversive, materialistic and seeking to rule the entire world as written in their holy book *the Talmud.*

Now, in the 21st Century, it really is amazing this international Jewish conspiracy theory, which has been shown to be fictitious over and over, remains such a popular delusion.

Could it be those of this era still subscribing to this theory do not realize they are recycling an ancient narrative that has been told and retold, and one that is based on nothing but old wives' tales, xenophobia and religious fanaticism?

Even at the very dawn of Christianity, there was a commonly-accepted theory known as *the Blood Libel,* which stated matter-of-factly that Jewish people regularly sacrificed non-Jewish babies and used the blood of those babies in Judaic rituals.

Later, in medieval times, plagues and other diseases were commonly blamed on Jews, resulting in the enforcement of Apartheid-like conditions, separating Jewish communities from the rest of the population throughout Europe. For example, in the Papal States –

Above: *'At the Feet of the Saviour',*
Slaughter of the Jews in the Middle Ages.

Painting by Vicente Cutanda y Toraya (1850–1925).

By Vicente Cutanda y Toraya –

The Bridgeman Art Library, Object 186996.

Licensed under Public Domain via Wikimedia Commons

territories in the Italian Peninsula that existed throughout the middle ages and medieval times that were governed directly by the Pope – Jews were only allowed to reside in neighborhoods called *ghettos*. They were regularly forced to convert to Christianity in various barbaric ways such as involuntary baptisms. The stealing of Jewish babies from their parents by Church officials was also not uncommon and the children would often then be brought up as Catholic orphans never knowing of their Jewish heritage.

An early anti-Semitic book, *On the Jews and Their Lies,* clearly illustrates the intentions of Catholic and Christian leaders of the era toward Jewish populations. Published in 1543 and written by Martin Luther, the German Reformation leader and one-time senior member of the Late Medieval Catholic Church, the book advocated killing all Jews who refused to convert to Christianity. In this regard, Luther wrote, "we are at fault in not slaying them". The Nazis would later cite this book to justify their perverse racial ideology and imply extermination of the Jews was God-inspired.

At times during the medieval era and even later, the Catholic Church continued to blame the Jews for killing Jesus Christ, and almost any affliction Catholics faced were said to be because of this ethno-religious minority. Some Catholic leaders even went as far as stating Jews were metaphorically re-enacting Jesus' crucifixion in their supposed attempts to undermine the Catholic faith.

Centuries later, in 1933, Adolf Hitler referenced the history of the Catholic Church's systematic persecution of Jews during a meeting with Roman Catholic Bishop Wilhelm Berning (de) of Osnabrück.

Hitler told Bishop Berning, "I have been attacked because of my handling of the Jewish question. The Catholic Church considered the Jews pestilent for fifteen hundred years, put them in ghettos, etc., because it recognized the Jews for what they were. In the epoch of liberalism the danger was no longer recognized. I am moving back toward the time in which a fifteen-hundred-year-long tradition was implemented. I do not set race over religion, but I recognize the representatives of this race as pestilent for the state and for the Church, and perhaps I am thereby doing Christianity a great service by pushing them out of schools and public functions."

Perhaps rather tellingly, in the transcript of this discussion between Hitler and the Roman Catholic leader, no response to the Führer's stated intentions towards the Jews or his assessment of Catholicism's history in dealing with Jews was made by Bishop Berning...

"Nazi anti-Judaism was the work of godless, anti-Christian criminals. But it would not have been possible without the almost two thousand years pre-history of 'Christian' anti-Judaism."

–*Hans Küng,* On Being a Christian

Whoever it was who said history repeats itself must have been talking about the history of the Jews as there have been numerous genocides of Jewish people throughout the centuries before the Holocaust. They include:

- In 70 A.D. the Roman army destroyed Jerusalem *and* killed one million Jews *and* also took 100,000 Jews as slaves.

- In the three-year Bar Kochba revolt against the Roman Empire that began in 132 AD, the Romans killed a half-million Jews and sold thousands of survivors into slavery.

- In 1298, more than 100 Jewish communities were destroyed in Austria, Bavaria and Franconia, resulting in the murder of at least 100,000 Jews.

- Hundreds of thousands of Jews were slaughtered during the Vatican-sanctioned Crusades (in which the Jewish people were the Christians' secondary target after the Muslims) in medieval times.

- Hundreds of thousands of Jews were killed during the Black Death (1347-49) – a plague which Judaism was blamed for.

- In 1648-1649, some 100,000 Jews were murdered by anti-Semitic peasants during an uprising against Polish rule in Ukraine.

- In 1915, more than 600,000 Jews were forcibly moved from the western borders of Russia toward the interior, resulting in the deaths of some 100,000 through exposure and starvation.

- During the Bolshevik Revolution in 1917, the White Armies used the hoaxed document *The Protocols of the Learned Elders of Zion* to incite widespread slaughters of Jews; some 200,000 Jews were murdered in Ukraine alone.

Given all the centuries of hatred toward them, it is a miracle any Jews survived.

Consider the historical record and look at the mighty empires, regimes and civilizations the Jewish people have outlasted: Ancient Egypt, the Philistines, the Assyrian Empire, the Babylonian Empire, the Persian Empire, the Greek Empire, the Roman Empire, the Byzantine Empire, the Crusaders, the Spanish Empire, the Soviet Union and the Third Reich. All have crumbled one way or another and none remain today.

And yet, against all odds, the Jewish people – a tiny community in the scheme of things – are still here, punching above their weight.

Those who belittle their immense suffering are not only heartless, they are also historically ignorant because the 20th Century – bad though it was for the Jews – was not necessarily the worst century for these people. Almost every century since Biblical times has been tumultuous and bloody, and a bitter fight to simply survive against enemies intent on eradicating them.

American history has not been immune to far-fetched, anti-Semitic theories that stated or implied the same tiny minority was pulling the strings of world affairs.

In 1934, it was alleged that one of the Founding Fathers of the United States, Benjamin Franklin, implored his contemporaries in a written statement at the 1787 Constitutional Convention to refuse Jews to be admitted into America, stating all the usual anti-Semitic reasons. Those reasons included the fallacy that Jews refused to assimilate in whichever country they resided in and that they would eventually rule the US and control its money supply.

Above: *Early 20th Century Jewish victims in a pogrom.*
Ekaterinoslav, Ukraine, 1905.
Photo distributed by Poale Zion
Licensed under Public Domain via Wikimedia Commons

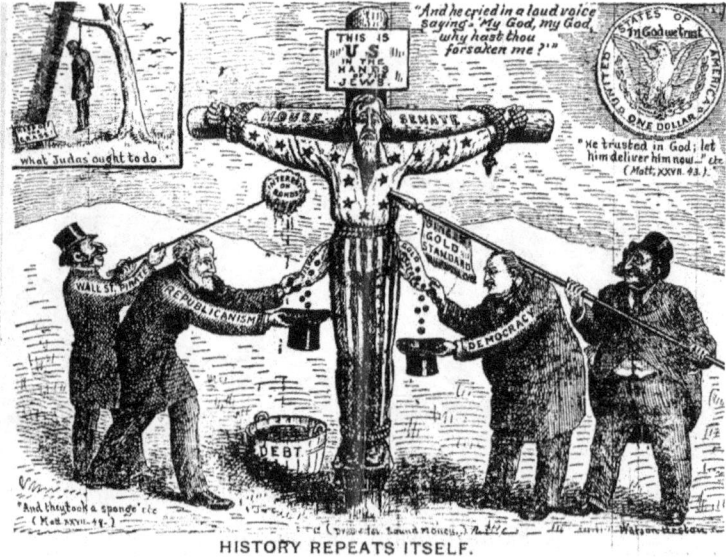

Above: *An 1896 anti-Semitic political cartoon portraying Uncle Sam being crucified by Jews like Jesus Christ. Licensed under Public Domain via Wikimedia Commons*

This alleged statement of Franklin's became known in US white supremacist circles as *the Franklin Prophecy*. An American magazine even published Franklin's rumored written excerpt as if it was a verified statement.

Soon afterward, the Anti-Defamation League (ADL) exposed Franklin's so-called *statement* as a fraud – and from the 1950s onwards all mainstream historians concur. Language experts have also studied the Franklin Prophecy and stated the excerpt contains anachronisms that Benjamin Franklin, who died in 1790, could never have written.

However, the Franklin Prophecy continues to be repeated all over the Internet and in conspiracy circles as if it's legitimate and in Franklin's own words.

Another anti-Semitic falsehood that has unfortunately reached legendary status in white supremacist communities is *The Protocols of the Learned Elders of Zion*. This 1903 treatise has potentially incited more anti-Semitism than any other hoax document. It also appears to have partly influenced the Nazis given it was required reading in all German schools for a time.

The Protocols spills the beans on a supposed global secret society of Jewish people planning world domination. From 1921 onwards, the dissertation has been unequivocally proven to be a falsified document written by anti-Semites. Yet today, almost a century later, it is still widely circulated by gullible conspiracy theorists as "undeniable proof" of the "Joooz controlling the world." Or was it controlling the entire universe? We forget.

Even automobile manufacturer Henry Ford, who, as mentioned in chapter 3, had close ties with the Nazis and was Hitler's biggest American financier, fell for the *Protocols* hoax. He went so far as to publish the tract in his own newspaper, *The Dearborn Independent*. Ford's widely distributed articles on the *Protocols*, and his printing of other anti-Semitic articles he and others wrote, eventually led to a collection of Ford's endorsements being published in a book titled *The International Jew: The World's Foremost Problem*.

"I would call it an intellectual disease, a disease of the mind, extremely infectious and massively destructive. It is a disease to which both human individuals and entire human societies are prone. What strikes the historian surveying anti-Semitism worldwide over more than two millennia is its fundamental irrationality. It seems to make no sense, any more than malaria or meningitis makes sense. In the whole of history, it is hard to point to a single occasion when a wave of anti-Semitism was provoked by a real Jewish threat (as opposed to an imaginary one). Like many physical diseases, anti-Semitism is highly infectious, and can become endemic in certain localities and societies. Though a disease of the mind, it is by no means confined to weak, feeble, or commonplace intellects; as history sadly records, its carriers have included men and women of otherwise powerful and subtle thoughts."

–Paul Johnson, *The Anti-Semitic Disease*

Above: Inspired by 'Protocols of the Elders of Zion'
(Spain, 1930).

By Anonymous – Protocolos de los sabios de Sion,

Licensed under Public Domain via Wikimedia Commons

Above: *An illustration of the dangers of the Internet generation?*

By Luigi Novi, CC BY 3.0,

https://commons.wikimedia.org/w/index.php?curid=16464308

Licensed under Public Domain via Wikimedia Commons

There was also an anti-Semitic twist on the ever-popular Illuminati conspiracy theory. For a brief period between the First and Second World Wars, as fascism advanced, various rampant fascists said the Illuminati was comprised solely of elite Jewish individuals who, they claimed, were dividing Europe to gain financial control and create a Jewish type of New World Order. It's possible this version of the Illuminati theory helped create a furtive and fertile environment to enable the likes of the Nazi Party to assume power so easily.

Other groups promoting the general idea that Jews are undermining democracy and that there is a secret Jewish or Zionist cabal ruling the planet include:

- Fundamentalist Christians of racist leanings who claim the anti-Christ will be a Jew and *the End Times* are intimately linked with Jewish money men.

- Neo-Nazis.

- Far Right Tea Party-style voters.

- Islamic extremists who regularly cite the *Protocols of the Elders of Zion* and claim either the Jewish population and/or Zionists are Islam's biggest enemy.

"We agree with his (Mel Gibson's) comments that the Jews started all wars. We also have proof that they were responsible for killing off all the dinosaurs. And Hurricane Katrina – they did it."

–Sacha Baron Cohen, publicizing his film Borat: Cultural Learnings of America for Make Benefit Glorious Nation of Kazakhstan

Still more conspiracy theorists claim the Jews are in control of the Freemasons, the New World Order, the capitalists *and* the communists, the Democrats *and* the Republicans, the Vatican, the United Nations, the British Royal Family and the White House.

If anti-Semitism hadn't been responsible for so much murder, destruction and suffering over the centuries, this loony conspiracy theory of Jewish global domination (in all its variations) would be hilarious due to its stupidity.

In a similar way to how the Catholic Church blamed the Jewish people for almost any problem within Catholic society in medieval times, modern anti-Semitic conspiracy extremists often say "Jewsdidit" to explain anything they cannot adequately explain in the world.

When paranoia reaches these levels, and such crackpot theories are accepted as if they are proven facts, it becomes relatively easy within such confused and hateful minds to accept that the Holocaust was wildly exaggerated after WW2 – or that it is even an entirely fictitious event that's been blamed on "the poor, misunderstood Nazis". An event in which the uber-powerful "Joooz" somehow pulled the strings of *every* mainstream historian, not to mention forensics experts and hundreds of thousands of Holocaust eyewitnesses, to fit their "convenient story" that a genocide occurred.

"The Jews started it all—and by 'it' I mean so many of the things we care about, the underlying values that make all of us, Jew and Gentile, believer and atheist, tick. Without the Jews, we would see the world through different eyes, hear with different ears, even feel with different feelings ... we would think with a different mind, interpret all our experience differently, draw different conclusions from the things that befall us. And we would set a different course for our lives."

—Thomas Cahill, The Gifts of the Jews

EIGHT

MYTH #7: "I have seen various figures thrown around regarding the number of Jews who died in Europe. It's hard to know which statistic to believe! There is almost no unbiased data about this subject! The way Jews play with the statistics, increasing the number of fatalities every year or so, is evidence of the Holocaust being more of a Holohoax!"

—Anonymous Holocaust denier #7

Death tolls of all wars and genocides are always estimates and cannot ever be 100% precise. For example, nobody can estimate how many precisely died in the Vietnam War. (Some historians say three million Vietnamese and 58,000 Americans, others say 3.2 million Vietnamese and 65,000 Americans).

There will always be slight variances in death tolls of any war, especially ones spanning entire continents and especially if you go as far back as WW2.

However, these slight variances are not supporting evidence for the facile arguments of Holocaust deniers who are simply looking for any avenue possible to try to revise history to support their hate-filled agendas.

Remember, deniers claim 90 to 100% of all Holocaust deaths are some fantasy concocted years after the war.

Rest assured the only books anywhere that talk about the tiny death toll numbers deniers believe in (i.e. tens of thousands or hundreds of thousands instead of millions) are Holocaust-denying books written by anti-Semitic "historians," religious zealots or neo-Nazis.

No mainstream history books ever published since 1945 mention a death toll that isn't in the millions for the Holocaust. Period.

To deny the reported six million (approximately) Jews who died, or the 11 million people in total, is to ignore all the eyewitness accounts from Holocaust survivors, the non-Jewish witnesses of the millions who died the open-air massacres around Europe, the concentration camp guards, Nazi officers who admitted to gassings and other related crimes immediately after WW2, and the universal agreement of *all* mainstream historians who have studied this historical event inside out – not to mention *every* single scientist who has *ever* analyzed forensic evidence retrieved from the Nazi genocide.

Not even the most corrupt courtroom on Earth could ignore this much evidence – for collectively these confirmations of the Holocaust equate to irrefutable proof that the reported death toll is indeed correct.

It is possibly the most well-documented crime of the 20th Century, but remember for religious extremists, Nazi apologists or other anti-Semites it would never matter how much evidence you put in front of them. They would always deny the Holocaust because to admit the event occurred would be to stop believing the Jews are inferior to them. It would also require such bigots to admit the very uncomfortable truth to themselves: that their 'own kind' did these despicable things to the Jewish people.

Another common argument the deniers bring up is the death toll relating to Auschwitz – a concentration camp where there have been conflicting reports about the number of those murdered.

Specifically, deniers often bring up the *Breitbard Document*, a paper by Aaron Breitbart who draws attention to a commemorative plaque at Auschwitz. This plaque, as the deniers repeatedly and triumphantly point out, did indeed read, "Four million people suffered and died here at the hands of the Nazi murderers between the years 1940 and 1945."

This overestimation of the number of deaths at Auschwitz was the result of Soviet propaganda. According to the Simon Wiesenthal Center, the Soviets "purposely overstated the number of non-Jewish casualties at Auschwitz-Birkenau."

The old plaque Breitbart referred to has long since been replaced. It now reads: "May this place where the Nazis assassinated 1,500,000 men, women and children, a majority of them Jews from diverse European countries, be forever for mankind a cry of despair and of warning."

Deniers claim this revised plaque is an admission that the death toll statistics were initially exaggerated and that the new plaque at Auschwitz reveals that the six million figure should be reduced by 2.5 million people.

However, what deniers miss, or perhaps purposefully ignore, is that the original plaque, based on the Soviet propaganda, was never used as an accurate historical source by mainstream historians. Nor was it included in the six million figure.

For example, Austrian-born American historian Raul Hilberg, widely considered to be the world's preeminent scholar of the Holocaust, was stating as early as the 1950s that approximately 1.1 million Jewish people died in Auschwitz.

Most deniers never research the Holocaust deeply enough to appreciate this nuance of WW2 historical reports, although there are some who are well aware of the truth, but decide to conceal it from their legion of followers to further their anti-Semitic aims.

And as for the idea that there is a Jewish conspiracy to increase the numbers of fatalities each year, then consider the 1989 publication of *Encyclopedia of the Holocaust*, by Israel Gutman, in which it's estimated total losses from 5,596,029 to 5,860,129. This roughly matches current estimates.

So, if the "global Jewish cabal" are increasing the death toll year after year, then why hasn't the estimated death toll increased in the decades that have elapsed since publication of the *Encyclopedia of the Holocaust* and similar mainstream history books of that era and earlier?

Another crucial thing to question is why deniers even bother to quibble about the number of deaths. If one day it were proven *only* five million or 5.5 million

Above: *Deceased found at the Buchenwald camp.*
Photo taken by Belgian war volunteer Jules Rouard.
CC BY-SA 3.0
https://commons.wikimedia.org/w/index.php?curid=316137
Licensed under Public Domain via Wikimedia Commons

Above: *Corpses found near the Jasenovac extermination camp, 1945.*

By United States Holocaust Memorial Museum, courtesy of Muzej Revolucije Narodnosti Jugoslavije

http://www.ushmm.org [Photograph #85196]

Licensed under Public Domain via Wikimedia Commons

Jews were exterminated, would it be any less an atrocity? What number would deniers suggest is low enough to say that genocide didn't occur and that it's not important that humanity remembers the Holocaust and the lessons learnt?

For example, a Holocaust denier wrote (using a pseudonym) the following to us on social media in relation to the exaggeration he assumes has occurred regarding the number of Jewish deaths: "We know terrible things happened, even without exaggerating, but exaggeration is still wrong. Not only because it is inaccurate, but because it sets a standard against which new atrocities are measured. New war criminals can always say, well what we are doing is still not as bad as the Holocaust. This alone makes it worth looking at whether all the deaths were really murders or whether many of them were indirect consequences of a bad policy and the general collapse in Germany as the war turned to defeat."

Could it be, yet again, such deniers have no real argument to offer and are simply trying to find minor anomalies in Holocaust records in order to purposefully distort and undermine history?

NINE

THE ISRAELI CONNECTION

MYTH #8: "Israel receives tremendous support from the United States and is therefore always shielded and immune from criticism. There are many Israeli policies that deserve to be criticized, some of which are downright fascist, but because of the fear everyone has of being labelled anti-Semitic, it becomes difficult to have a rational discussion about topics that really should be addressed. And this is all intimately connected with the suppression of truths surrounding the supposed gas chambers because Israel has greatly benefitted from the big lie that is the 'official story' of the Holocaust."

—Anonymous Holocaust denier #8

Issues like the Middle East conflict, Israeli-Palestinian relations and Zionism are often, and quite incorrectly, brought into discussions about the Holocaust. (Zionism, incidentally, can loosely be

DEBUNKING HOLOCAUST DENIAL THEORIES

defined in the 21st Century as nationalism or patriotism relating to the state of Israel).

These more recent and predominantly regional conflicts and issues are not remotely related to an event that happened in Europe before and during a world war that occurred before the independent state of Israel was even formed. And yet the deniers mischievously continue to endeavor to link Zionism and the aforementioned conflicts with the Holocaust in their efforts to undermine the historicity of that event.

The aforementioned United States Holocaust Memorial Museum article titled *Origins of Holocaust Denial* references this very denial theory as follows:

"Many people who deny the Holocaust argue that the supposed 'hoax' served above all the interests of the State of Israel. Holocaust denial is, for these people, also an attack on the legitimacy of the State of Israel."

In his 1964 article titled *Zionist Fraud*, published in the renowned anti-Semitic magazine *American Mercury*, US fringe historian and Holocaust denier Harry Elmer Barnes lays "the chief blame for misrepresentation on those whom we must call the swindlers of the crematoria, the Israeli politicians who derive billions of marks from nonexistent, mythical and imaginary cadavers, whose numbers have been reckoned in an unusually distorted and dishonest manner."

Since Barnes' article, numerous other anti-Semitic authors and self-proclaimed historians have repeated the myth that the Holocaust is a fabrication or gigantic exaggeration by Israelis for the good of Israel.

For example, the ADL reported one modern Holocaust denier, Bradley Smith, wrote in the *Outlaw*

History Newsletter that "The entire Israeli enterprise is based on a mountain of fraud and greed."

For the record, Israel was created on May 14, 1948, almost three years to the day after WW2 officially ended. And more importantly, the historicity of the Holocaust – including the death toll, eyewitness accounts and confirmations of gas chambers – had already been cemented by historians well before Israel's formation date.

So how people can even consider let alone believe that Israel orchestrated the "official story" of the Holocaust beats us. Perhaps those who subscribe to the Israeli Holocaust hoax theory not only see Israel's eight million citizens as having God-like powers that enable them to secretly control other nation's historians, but also possessing time-machines that allow them to choreograph events to suit Israel *before* Israel was established!

Bringing up wrongdoings of the Israeli government is therefore about as relevant to the Holocaust as mentioning the warmongering decisions of recent US administrations in relation to the slaughter of Native Americans when America was first colonized centuries ago.

In other words, whatever your opinion of Israel's handling of the Middle East conflict – and we ourselves have some misgivings on that matter – that is in no way shape or form related to the facts of the Holocaust.

"While criticism of Israel is legitimate and justifiable, it cannot be an excuse - in any way, shape or form - for anti-Semitism."

–Tariq Ramadan

Above: *David Ben-Gurion (Israel's First Prime Minister) pronouncing the Declaration of State of Israel, Tel Aviv, 1948. By Rudi Weissenstein - Israel Ministry of Foreign Affairs Licensed under Public Domain via Wikimedia Commons*

We do of course agree that as Israel is just another country, and not a race or religion, anybody should be able to criticize the country all they like. Israel already receives considerable censure from critics and from the world's media. But even *if* there are sensitivities around delivering criticism of Israel, these would still remain totally separate to the issues of the Holocaust and verifying that the Nazi genocide, which *again* pre-dates Israel, occurred as historians and verified documents attest.

So, bringing Israel and modern Zionism into the subject of the Holocaust is to bring current (i.e. *late* 20th and early 21st Century) issues into a historical event that occurred on another continent altogether in the *early-mid* 20th Century.

> *"Deniers build their pseudo-arguments on traditional anti-Semitic stereotypes and imagery. They contend that Jews created the myth of the Holocaust in order to bilk the Germans out of billions of dollars and ensure the establishment of Israel. Once again the devious Jews have harmed innocent multitudes—Germans and Palestinians in particular—for the sake of their own financial and political ends. To someone nurtured by the soil of anti-Semitism, this makes perfect sense."*
>
> *–Deborah E. Lipstadt,* The Eichmann Trial

It's also worth pointing out that Israel is not solely comprised of Jewish people and is *not* the defining representation of the global Jewish community. There are many non-Jewish Israelis – about 25% of Israeli citizens are non-Jewish and mostly Muslim with some

Christians – and of course there are many non-Israeli Jews, including American Jews for example.

However, the above statistics are either underreported or lost in the paranoiac thinking so common to those who assess such disparate subjects as Jewish people, Zionism, Judaism, Israel and the Holocaust as if they are all one and the same and inextricably linked. The all-too-real problem of rising anti-Semitism around the world is unfortunately often a result of anti-Zionist or anti-Israeli beliefs. This phenomenon can usually be traced to the blurring of the lines or general confusion in gentiles and their apparent inability in the main to differentiate between the global Jewish community and the distinctly different and separate nation of Israel.

Consider the following emailed to us by an anti-Semite obsessed with the idea of a supposed mega-conspiracy of Zionists/Israelis/Jews profiting from the aftermath of the Nazi genocide:

"I admire your passion and idealism on this issue. It reminds me a lot of the way I felt about it 40 years ago, when I knew of no alternative narrative to the mainstream, Hollywood, Zionist, or official schoolbook version. It is more complicated than that. There are Jews who oppose Zionism, there are Christian Zionists. It is not all black and white or one sided. I see a lot more shades of gray now. None of these alternative viewpoints change the fact that a terrible and unjust punishment was meted out to innocent Jews in WW2. But they were not the only victims of that war, in which tens of millions died. Why is THE Holocaust raised to the status of the Holiest of Holies? There is an agenda behind that and it is not pretty. It is used to justify the usurpation of Palestine

Above: *A protestor in Melbourne, Australia purposefully blurring the lines between WW2 historical fact and an opinion of current events?*

By Takver - originally posted to Flickr as Melbourne Gaza protest: Zionist Criminals, End the Palestine Holocaust,

CC BY-SA 2.0,

Licensed under Public Domain via Wikimedia Commons

Above: *Anti-Zionist graffiti (or is it anti-Semitic??).*
By zombie of zombietime.com, CC BY 3.0
http://www.zombietime.com/sf_rally_february_16_2003/,
Licensed under Public Domain via Wikimedia Commons

and the ongoing genocide against native peoples in the Middle East. It props up the entire Anglo-Zionist scheme for world domination. Thus you are going to have people inspecting it for weak spots, for a foothold in the battle against the New World Order's war on humanity."

This more recent and more complex paranoia about Jews and Zionism was addressed by UCLA student Arielle Mokhtarzadeh in an article dated May 24, 2015, in *The Huffington Post*. Writing as a first-year student, she perceptively comments on "the rise of what has become known as the new anti-Semitism."

Ms Mokhtarzadeh states: "Although we would like to believe much has changed since the 18th Century, in regards to anti-Semitism, it has not...We (Jews) are forced 'not to be so public' about our Jewish identities. We are expected to be experts on all facets of Judaism and explain them on cue. We are assumed to be blind supporters of the Jewish state and manifestations of its government.

"And between combating Divestment resolutions, defending ourselves against anti-Semitism and constantly trying to afford our peers context, we have lost sight of what we really came to these universities for: an education...

"With the newest incessant barrage of anti-Israel legislation creeping into student governments across the country, anti-Israel rhetoric has slowly but surely transformed college campuses into breeding grounds for false perceptions of Jews and their beliefs.

"The systematic singling out, delegitimization, demonization and setting of double standards in relation to the Jewish state has led to the systematic singling out, delegitimization, demonization and setting of double standards in relation to the Jewish people."

Ms Mokhtarzadeh gives examples, including "discrimination at UCLA," a call for expulsion of some Jewish students at the University of Durban in South Africa, and the presence of swastikas at the University of California Davis, Emory University and "most recently" George Washington University.

"Disdain for Israeli policy or decisions of the Israeli government are never an excuse for anti-Semitism," she writes. "In their pervasive crusade against the Jewish state, the world has renewed an age-old, historic hatred against the Jewish people."

We can only echo her plea: "It is essential that we put an end to it now."

When it comes to criticism of the United States deciding to protect Israel, perhaps President Obama is the best one to answer that.

In a January 19, 2016 article in *The Washington Post*, Obama cites "the words of an American World War II hero" proclaiming that "Christians and people of other faiths can say 'we are all Jews' in solidarity."

The article reads, "The president made his remark during a ceremony at the Israeli Embassy in Washington, where he took part in the first Righteous Among Nations awards banquet held in the United States...

" 'Here, tonight, we must confront the reality that around the world, anti-Semitism is on the rise. We cannot deny it,' Obama said. 'An attack on any faith is an attack on all of our faiths...When voices around the world veer from criticism of a particular Israeli policy to an unjust denial of Israel's right to exist, when Israel faces terrorism, we stand up forcefully and proudly in defense of our ally, in defense of our friend, in defense of the Jewish state of Israel,' Obama said."

The Washington Post article concludes, " 'America's commitment to Israel's security remains, now and forever, unshakable. And I've said this before -- it would be a fundamental moral failing if America broke that bond...I cannot imagine a greater expression of Christianity than to say, I, too, am a Jew,' Obama said. 'When any Jew anywhere is targeted just for being Jewish, we all have to respond'."

TEN

MYTH #9: "Elite (atheistic) Jews, who were all Zionists hellbent on creating a Jewish homeland, created the Holocaust for their own gain. These Zionists, like the Rothschild family, secretly pulled the strings of the Nazis to orchestrate millions of Jews being slaughtered in an effort to create enough international sympathy to form the nation of Israel (a plan which obviously succeeded)."

—Anonymous Holocaust denier #9

If you think this sounds like the most outlandish conspiracy theory ever dreamed up about the Holocaust, you're probably not wrong.

This particular myth deniers promote is the oddest of all as many (deniers) are essentially conceding the Holocaust occurred as per modern historians' assessment in terms of the gassings and even the death toll. *But* here's the rub: the Jews, not the Nazis, masterminded the Holocaust!

Yes, you read that right. This zany theory would have us believe Hitler and the Nazis were simply used as pawns to carry out the genocide plan of these evil, wealthy, Jewish elites.

Confused? You're not alone!

High profile promoters of this bizarre Zionist-creation-of-the-Holocaust theory include former president of Iran Mahmoud Ahmadinejad, Palestinian President Mahmoud Abbas and the Institute for Historical Review to name but a few, but more about them later.

Meanwhile, allow us to attempt to break down this Zionist genocide creation myth or conspiracy, whichever description you prefer.

As we understand it, this was supposedly a multi-tiered conspiracy that occurred over several decades from the dawn of modern Zionism until after WW2.

The alleged timeline of events looks something like this:

1. Zionism was formed as an official political movement in the late 1800's with the goal of eventually creating a Jewish nation in the land that is now Israel.

2. By the early 20th Century, the global Jewish community, who at that time predominantly resided in Europe and the US, did not want to move to the Middle East despite the Zionists' best efforts to entice them. Most Jews were happy to remain where they were born or had settled. At this point (in the eyes of those who subscribe to this theory we would remind you!) Jews and Muslims all got along, as did Jews and

Christians, so there was no obvious reason or motivation for Jews to relocate to Israel as apparently anti-Semitism was not a big problem.

3. As there were no signs the Jewish populace would ever relocate of their own volition, Zionist banking dynasties like the Rothschild family in Europe and industry tycoons in the US devised an evil and ultimately bloody plan to encourage them to move there.

4. This Zionist cabal financed and helped clear the path for Hitler's war machine for the dual purpose of making truckloads of money by financing both sides in the war while, at the same time, engineering the Holocaust in order to scare surviving Jews to move to Israel.

5. After initially promising Hitler and the Nazis they would support them to the death, the Zionists then turned against the Germans and cleared the path once more – this time for the Allies to come in, save the surviving Jews and loudly announce to the world that the genocide that was the Holocaust *had* really occurred.

6. The international sympathy for the Jewish people was by this stage overwhelming, and the Zionists were then able to convince the international community to "turn a blind eye" as they *illegally* steamrolled into the Middle East and seized the Holy Land to create a Jewish nation.

7. After the Holocaust, surviving Jewish people were now only too happy to move to a protected homeland created for them, and the Zionists

found it was easy to manipulate these remaining Jews to relocate by presenting the relocation as "freedom".

8.   And voilà: You have Israel!

Boy, do these deniers make a lot of assumptions. Not sure if they realize it, but they do come across as tinfoil-hat-wearing conspiracy extremists. You know the ones...They wear hats made out of aluminum foil to protect the brain from such threats such as mind control and electromagnetic fields.

We suggest they'd be better off adhering to *Occam's razor* – that 14th Century philosophical principle, which suggests the simplest explanation with the least amount of *assumptions* is usually the correct one.

The idea that a small group of elite Jewish bankers and businessmen pulled the strings of fascist politicians in the 1920s and 1930s, *and* that was the sole reason Hitler and his cronies took over Germany, *and* that was why the Nazis were able to establish the Third Reich (one of the most powerful empires in history remember), *and* Zionist support alone led to the Holocaust, which paved the way for the creation of Israel, is possibly the most highly-speculative, totally unproven and far-fetched connecting-the-dots-style conspiracy theory ever conjured up. Surely!

Tragically, this theory is often employed as a last ditch anti-Semitic effort by more educated deniers. The type who upon studying the Holocaust in-depth eventually realizes the weight of evidence for the genocide is overwhelming and beyond any shadow of doubt. Once that obvious truth sinks in, such deniers look for a way – *any* way – to convince themselves and others the "Jewsdidit".

And the theory that the Zionists were behind the Holocaust allows them to continue their hate-filled agendas. Sad isn't it?

As mentioned earlier, one promoter of the Zionist genocide creation myth is none other than one of the world's most well-known Holocaust deniers, the former president of Iran, Mahmoud Ahmadinejad, whose favorite saying (in Persian) is reportedly "Death to Israel."

In a speech given on the *IRINN* network on September 18, 2009, Ahmadinejad stated: "Anti-Semitism was planned mainly by some European governments and politicians, and by the Zionist network. They made hundreds of films, wrote hundreds of books, spread rumors, and conducted psychological warfare, in order to drive them away, to the land of Palestine. Four or five years after World War II, they suddenly claimed that during that war, the Holocaust affair had taken place. In other words, according to their claims, several million Jews were burned in the crematoria. They created two slogans. The first was about the injustice suffered by the Jewish people. By means of lies, very twisted propaganda, and psychological warfare, they created the notion that the Jews suffered injustice, and, secondly, that they needed a land and an independent state. They acted so effectively that some of the world's politicians and intellectuals were also deceived and influenced."

Palestinian President Mahmoud Abbas, who is the successor to Yasser Arafat, clearly shares similar thoughts in relation to the Zionists' role in the Holocaust. In 1982, President Abbas wrote his doctoral dissertation on the subject and titled it "The Secret Connection between the Nazis and the Leaders of the Zionist Movement." In that thesis, Abbas expressed his

Above: Early 20th Century USA cigarette silk with Zionist flag.
Center for Jewish History, NYC.
Licensed under Public Domain via Wikimedia Commons

belief that gas chambers were never used by Nazis to murder Jews.

The following year, Abbas' book *The Other Side: the Secret Relationship Between Nazism and Zionism* was published. It was an expanded version of his thesis, and in it Abbas not only denies that six million Jews died in the Holocaust, he also dismisses the Nazi genocide as a "fantastic lie" and summarizes it as a "myth." He claims the minor death toll had had been exaggerated by Zionists to further their agenda.

While later appearing to change his tune and acknowledge that the Holocaust did occur and was a terrible injustice against the Jewish people, Abbas remained true to the other aspect of his original thesis: that the Holocaust was a joint effort between Nazis *and* Zionists. In fact, in 2012, the Palestinian President told the Hezbollah-associated Beirut television station *Al Mayadeen* that he "challenges anyone who can deny that the Zionist movement had ties with the Nazis before World War Two."

Apart from being a fairly popular theory subscribed to in the Muslim world, it is also one regularly used by deniers in the West to shift blame away from the Nazis, white people or Catholics/Christians and instead solely blame Jews for the Holocaust.

Such bigotry is another way of saying, "Even *if* the Holocaust did happen as historians attest, the Rothschilds and other evil Zionists obviously created it all and therefore *Joooz* are still responsible either way – for the real genocide *or* the hoax version – and therefore it wasn't the Germans' fault as they were, of course, the real victims."

What is staggering is that this is one of the most subscribed-to Holocaust denial theories. Possibly that's because of the complexity of the theory.

Anti-Semites can be very crafty and adept at converting impressionable minds by obfuscating their bigotry with half-truths – such as their assertion that many in high finance and the banking elite are bastards. (Something more than a few of us would agree with no doubt). Such obfuscation can be problematic as most 9-5 workers in this world just don't have the time or inclination to extensively research history and fact-check obscure theories or alternative versions of history.

In truth, all that supports this particular Holocaust denial myth, and variations on it, are a few tiny pieces of evidence and nothing remotely resembling proof or the smoking gun deniers would have us believe they have uncovered. (Those leaning toward denialism shouldn't get too excited about our reference to evidence being found. Keep in mind *evidence* is only ever a fact that suggests something might be true, unlike proof, which is something that removes all doubt).

According to our research, up until the 1920s and even early 1930s, the likes of the Rothschilds and other Jewish banking elites channeled funds to the German government and to German/Swiss banks who were early supporters of the Nazi regime. And yes, some of the banking elites of the day were pushing for a Zionist nation (a modern version of ancient Israel) long before WW2.

However, conspiracy-minded researchers are drawing a mighty long bow if they expect anyone to believe a small group of bankers could pull the strings of the all-powerful Third Reich – an empire so powerful it took the combined might of the Soviets, British and Americans *and* all their allies around the world – to finally bring it down.

Incredibly, these same researchers (let's call them what they are – *conspiracy theorists*) imply the Zionists had crystal ball-like prophetic powers that enabled them to predict with absolute certainty that this fascist regime would not only eventually lose the war, but would also commit the Holocaust atrocity yet somehow leave enough Jews alive to be able to form the nation of Israel.

How would those orders be written up? "Kill a lot, but not too many" perhaps. Or "Kill six million, but no more."

Go figure!

There was also *massive* funding for the Nazis from the Vatican Bank. So how come nobody promotes an equivalent conspiracy theory stating the Catholics bankrolled the Nazis to create the Holocaust for their own devious purposes? Or they bankrolled them or to wipe the Jews off the face of the Earth in some fundamentalist echo of the Biblical era?

It's likely you could find as much "evidence" to support that theory quite easily – *if* that's the path you wanted to follow.

We have also taken the time to fact-check many quotes that have been attributed to members of the Rothschild family, including those that are being used to support this particular Holocaust denial myth. And 90% of these quotes have been fabricated, often by members of the Muslim fundamentalist community as well as by neo-Nazis or Nazi apologists. It's no coincidence that such false quotes paint a nasty picture of Zionism ruling our planet.

One of numerous examples of such quotes, or other people's quotes being wrongly attributed to the Rothschilds, is one that is cited all over the Internet and has even been published in books. Since 1935, it has been repeatedly claimed that Mayer Amschel Rothschild (1744–1812) once said: "Permit me to issue and control the money of a nation, and I care not who makes its laws!"

Historians not only agree there is no way to verify who made that statement, but they unanimously agree the quote is a rehashed version of a statement made by Scottish politician Andrew Fletcher (1655–1716) – before the Rothschild in question was even born!

Fletcher wrote the following oft-quoted remark in his 1703 book, *An Account of a Conversation concerning a right regulation of Governments for the common good of Mankind*: "If a man were permitted to make all the ballads, he need not care who should make the laws of a nation."

Alas, such salacious quotes by power-mad *gentiles* are not worth repeating or even correctly attributing to the individual...

What also strongly refutes the Zionist denial theory is that many of the Jewish bankers of the mid-20th Century (those "evil Zionist bankers") had to flee Germany and other European nations to avoid persecution by the Nazis. Undoubtedly, most of those bankers had the wealth and connections to obtain safe passage to the United States, Britain and elsewhere to avoid becoming victims of the Holocaust, but the point is they still had to flee. This fact directly contradicts that wacky theory that elite Jewish bankers (often

Above: *Mayer Amschel Rothschild – wrongly quoted?*
From The Jewish Encyclopedia printed in 1907.
Licensed under Public Domain via Wikimedia Commons

nicknamed Zionist-*expletives* all over the Internet) were in bed with the Nazis or even controlling the entire Third Reich so they could create the Holocaust.

Further undermining this particular denial theory is that not all members of the Jewish banking elite avoided the wrath of the Nazis.

For example, Élisabeth de Rothschild (1902-1945) died in the Holocaust after being captured by the Gestapo in France whilst trying to flee the Nazis. Élisabeth was sent to Ravensbrück concentration camp where she died.

In a less violent but still valid example, Louis Nathaniel de Rothschild, of Austria, is a Holocaust survivor who was imprisoned for a period after his property was seized in 1938, and he lost all his assets including the family's palace. Louis also had a hard fight hard to achieve freedom from the Nazis for his (Jewish) wife and children.

Let's face it, Rothschild Holocaust theories and similar beliefs about "evil Zionist bankers" are yet another way for anti-Semites and deniers of the Nazi genocide to distract from the historical facts.

Again, we are not trying to defend, or even comment on, the overall financial empire of the Rothschilds or the way they conduct their operations – that is all a totally separate matter. Nor do we support any of the banking elite (Jewish or non-Jewish) for that matter. Just because the Rothschilds are Jewish does not mean they are *for* the Jewish people. For all we know, the Rothschilds may be elitists first and foremost, their primary religion may be money not Judaism, and their ethnicity may be the color of money. In other words, they *may* have no allegiance to any nation or community of people whatsoever.

Just because George W. Bush, Barack Obama and Tony Blair are all Christians or Catholics, does that mean we should assume everything they say and do is representative of their religion or is on behalf of their faith or denomination? That makes no more sense than suggesting everything those three individuals do is on behalf of all white people or all black people.

Keep in mind there are always certain races or followers of certain religions or doctrines who dominate specific fields. So yes, there are many Jewish banking clans to be found in the world of high finance. But if you stop to think about it, why is it the deniers single out Jews and the banking field only?

We would estimate 95% of what is termed the 'ruling elite' or global elite – the so-called 1% whose members include the likes of World Bank executives, Bilderbergers, senior CIA staffers and British Royals – are white and Christian. And maybe 60% or so are also American.

So, why aren't those deniers who single out the Jews and who state or imply that "Joooz control the world" saying "Whites control Mother Earth and wage war against non-whites, and the world we live in is the result of white supremacy" – and why aren't they saying that "Christianity is trying to destroy all other religions" or that "the United States is the reason for all the world's problems and America is secretly running the entire world."???

The answer can once again be summarized in two words: anti-Semitism.

"Holocaust deniers claim that there is a vast conspiracy involving the victorious powers of World War II, Jews, and Israel to propagate the Holocaust for their own ends."

—*United States Holocaust Memorial Museum, HOLOCAUST DENIERS AND PUBLIC MISINFORMATION*

When it comes to debunking this "Zionists are responsible" Holocaust denial myth, we think the aforementioned and painstakingly-researched *Nizkor Project* handled it best in its reply to one of the most outlandish claims made by the Institute for Historical Review.

IHR, which is considered by most scholars to be the center of the international Holocaust denial movement, stated, "Before the war, Germany signed an agreement with the Zionists permitting Jews to take large amounts of capital to Palestine. During the war, the Germans maintained cordial relations with the Zionist leadership."

To which Nizkor replied as follows:

"Cordial relations? Now really. With a leadership that had declared publicly, again and again, that Jews are vermin that should be exterminated? ... This...seems to be another internal contradiction. They (IHR) say that "Judea" and "the Jews" declared war on Germany six years before World War II started. The IHR should make up its mind: either the Germans were vilified by the hateful Jews, or the Germans are such good people that even the hateful Jews were able to maintain "cordial relations" with them. They can't have it both ways."

ELEVEN

A MONTAGE OF THE "HOLOCAUST BY BULLETS"

MYTH #10: "You must remember Zionist bankers and Bolsheviks financed the Holodomor genocide of my people in the 1930s in which several million died. Fact: malicious Jewish Bolsheviks did that to my fellow Ukrainians. So you first need to understand the Ukrainian people were rightfully very angry at Jews for creating all these horrors in Ukraine and throughout Eastern Europe. However, overall, we Ukrainians were never anti-Semitic in the main. In fact, 99.9% of the atrocities in Ukraine committed against Jews were Nazis killing them, NOT us killing them. There are many untold stories of heroic Ukrainians rescuing Jews from harm, but you never hear about those stories. The Zionist-controlled media, who besides obfuscating the REAL facts about the Holocaust (e.g. the gas chamber deaths are greatly exaggerated), only ever reports those isolated cases where radical nationalists or far-Right Ukrainians, as well as the odd civilian, killed Jews in my country."

—Anonymous Holocaust denier #10

Isolated cases, huh?

And the "odd civilian," you say?

We beg to differ with you in your analysis of these genocides, and, more importantly, the weight of history is against you, too.

All mainstream historians agree that what caused the Holodomor (that Ukrainian genocide often referred to as the Famine-Genocide) was not Jewish or Zionist bankers, but rather a Russian dictator named Joseph Stalin (whose name may ring a bell?) and a colossal empire called the Soviet Union (which you also may have heard of?).

When it comes to the Holocaust, the history of Ukrainian civilians' involvement in the murders of Ukrainian Jews is proven to be much more common than the "isolated cases" you refer to. In reality, your countrymen were all too often accomplices of the Nazis for various reasons – sometimes they were forced to comply, but oftentimes they needed no prompting to slaughter their Jewish compatriots.

The historical truth is that almost a third of all Jews who perished in the Holocaust died on Ukrainian soil in open-air shootings. While most were killed by Germans, there were also a large number of Jewish victims killed in cold blood by ordinary Ukrainians, usually with, but sometimes without, Nazis on the scene giving orders.

So your statement that Ukrainians were not anti-Semitic in the main is not only delusional but ignorant of an extremely well-documented historical episode of WW2.

Ukraine was in many ways the epicenter of the genocide of Jews outside of the Nazis' concentration camps in Poland and other European countries.

Historians now estimate 1.6 million Jews were executed in Ukraine.

Referred to as the *Holocaust by Bullets*, or alternatively the *Holocaust of Bullets*, the Ukrainian atrocities were definitely Nazi-inspired and would not likely have occurred if it wasn't for the German invasion. However, to make the nationwide slaughter more efficient, the Germans utilized the anti-Semitic undercurrent in the Ukrainian population who, as outlined in chapter 7, committed genocides against Jews in earlier decades and earlier centuries. History shows that before the Third Reich invaded the region there had already been numerous violent pogroms against the Jewish population in various Ukrainian cities.

By all accounts, the Nazis did not come up against much resistance from the local population in their desire to eradicate Ukrainian Jews. Of course, it is much more complicated than that as it is well-documented that many Ukrainians were forced to aid the Nazis in the killings. Oftentimes it was a case of kill or be killed.

We also want to add we are not anti-Ukrainian. In fact, we suspect our DNA may reveal we have some Ukrainian ancestry ourselves. We are not about picking on any one nationality, but rather using Ukrainians as an example of how the stain of anti-Semitism in the early-mid 20th Century was almost Europe-wide and how that aided the Nazis in their efforts to implement their Jewish eradication plans. Nor do we wish to undermine or negate the fact that millions of Ukrainians died at the hands of the Nazis, which was a massive human tragedy in itself.

However, we also think all peoples everywhere must learn from history. Such learning – and by default such evolution – can only occur in a society when historical facts are acknowledged no matter how painful it may be to accept those facts.

To imply there were only ever isolated incidents where local Ukrainian citizens willingly tortured and murdered Jews is very, very wrong. Such implications, rumours or lies – call them what you will – appear to be nothing more than an attempt to revise history.

The atrocities in Ukraine were some of the most barbaric, brutal and systematic of the entire war. Even without the rest of the Holocaust, the nationwide slaughters of Jews in Ukraine alone would have gone down as one of the worst genocides in history.

An August 2015 article that appeared in Britain's *Daily Mail* does an excellent job of summarizing the shameful secrets of Ukraine's Holocaust by Bullets. It quotes local eyewitnesses as saying, "Blood oozed through the soil at grave sites," and "You could see the pits move, some of them were still alive."

The Daily Mail's report continues, "Seventy years on from the end of the Second World War the full, shocking scale of the Nazi-inspired Holocaust in Ukraine is finally being revealed ...Around 2,000 mass graves of Jewish victims have been located where men, women and children were shot and buried by the Germans and their collaborators. But there may be up to 6,000 more sites to uncover, with victims of this 'Holocaust of bullets' - so called because unlike in Poland and Germany where gas chambers were used as the means of slaughter - here most were summarily shot and buried nearby. In many cases, the Jews were ordered to dig pits and then to strip naked before they were mown down by their murderers. Some were buried in the unmarked plots while still alive."

The article goes on to confirm a sector of Ukrainian society did collaborate with the Nazis in attempting to eradicate all of the nation's Jews. "For modern Ukraine the subject is difficult, too, because it means admitting a role for nationalists in colluding with the Nazis."

The *Daily Mail* article also quotes Mikhail Tyaglyy, historian of the Ukrainian Centre of Holocaust Study, as saying, "We are touching the topic of Ukrainian nationalism here and it is a complicated matter. The situation in Ukraine was not so different to what was going on in other Soviet regions which were occupied by Nazis – everywhere they relied on local nationalists, who often blamed Jews for supporting the 'Moscow-Bolshevik regime'.

"Such attitudes easily inspired pogroms as we had in Western Ukraine. The Nazis did their best to inspire pogroms everywhere they came."

Tyaglyy is also quoted as saying, "It is true that radical (Ukrainian) nationalists helped Nazis in guarding and performed other tasks."

So, Anonymous Holocaust denier, we'd ask you to stop and ponder history properly before stating that Ukrainians barely participated at all in the persecution of Jews.

Implying that the accusations against Ukranian peoples' involvement in this part of the Holocaust are nothing but fabrications resulting from Zionist propaganda is actually modern Ukrainian (nationalistic) propaganda.

We trust the following photographic evidence taken exclusively in Ukraine during the Holocaust by Bullets will speak for itself and silence any debate about whether some locals willingly participated in the persecution and slaughter of Jews...

Above: *A Jewish man is kicked by a local during a pogrom in the Ukrainian city of Lviv in 1941. Public domain image*

Above: *A Jewish man yanked by the hair during the pogrom in Lviv, Ukraine, 1941.*

Public domain image

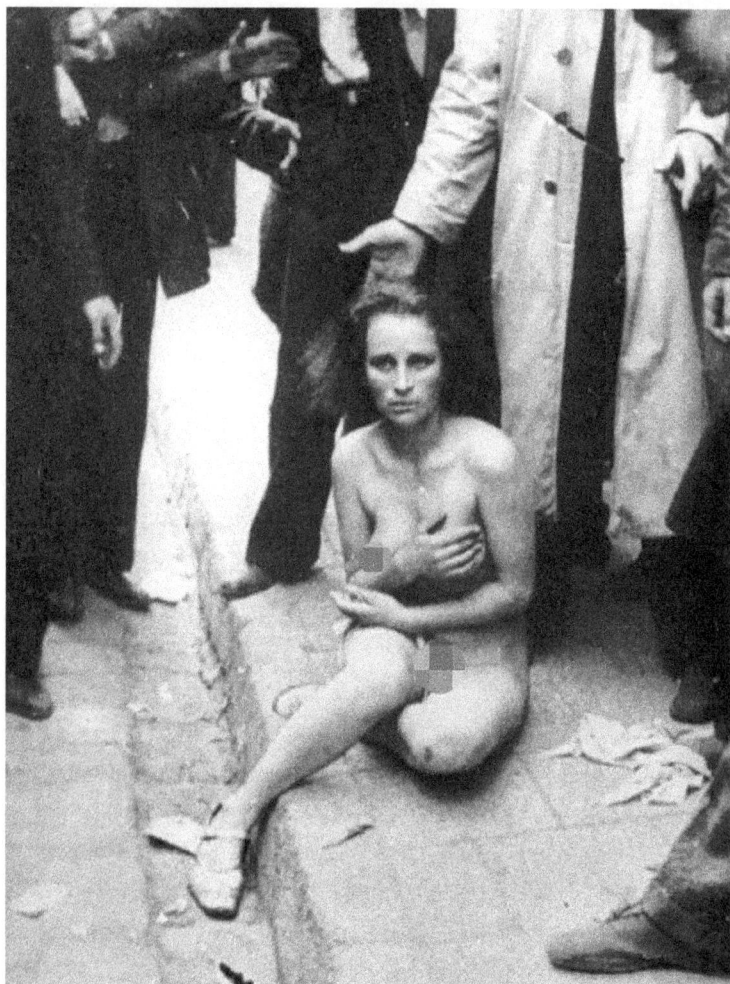

Above: *A Jewish woman is stripped naked as part of public humiliation.*

Lviv pogrom, Ukraine, 1941.

Public domain image

Above: *A Jewish mother tries to protect her naked daughter during a public humiliation.*

Lviv pogrom, 1941.

Public domain image

Above: *A severely-injured Jewish man struggles to stand up after being beaten in the 1941 Lviv pogrom.*

Public domain image

Above: *A Ukrainian mob rip a Jewish woman's clothes off in the street in a Nazi organized anti-Semitic riot (pogrom).*

Public domain image

Above: *Another Jewish victim of a Ukrainian pogrom.*
Public domain image

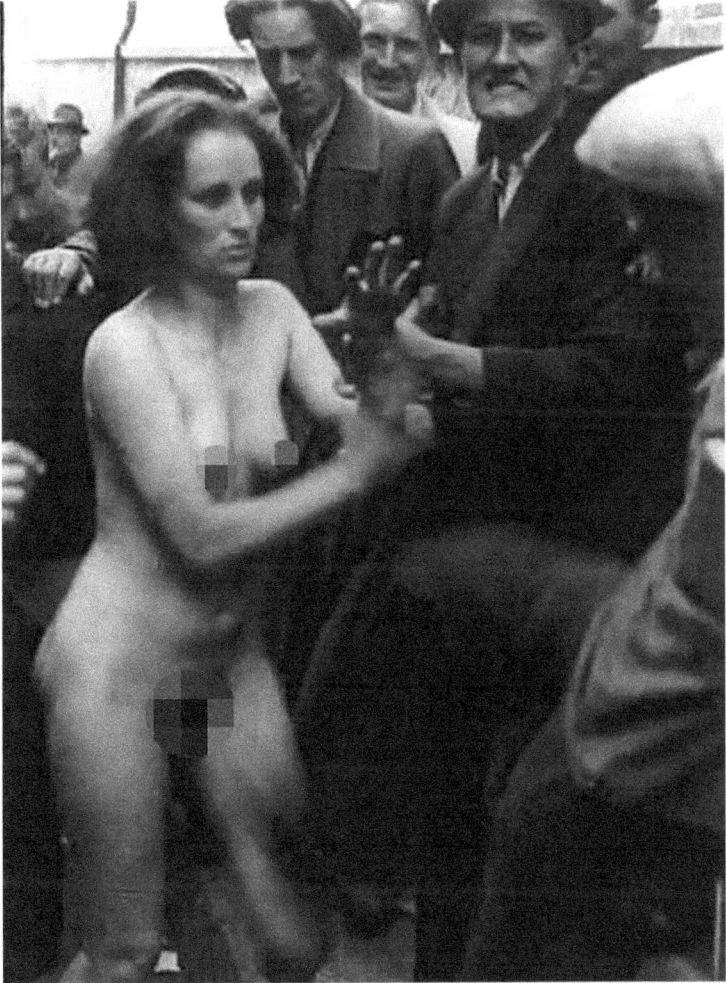

Above: *A Jewish lady humiliated during a pogrom in Lviv, 1941.*

Public domain image

Above: *More Jews under siege in Ukraine.*
Public domain image

Above: *The bloodied remains of Jewish victims after a night of violence at a pogrom in Ukraine.*

Public domain image

Above: *Blood reportedly oozed from the soil of mass graves of Jews (such as pictured above) all over Ukraine.*

Public domain image

Above: *A pile of bones discovered in the Ukrainian town of Belzec (near the site of four mass graves in Rava Ruska).*

Public domain image

WILL HISTORY FOREVER REPEAT ITSELF?

*"Only in our remembrance and open discussion
is there a chance, a hope, that another
Holocaust will never happen."*

−Louis Weber, publisher of The Holocaust Chronicle

"Never forget" is the collective plea of Holocaust survivors. And in the first few decades after WW2 ended, it really did seem as if humanity would always remember, and perhaps even learn from, the Nazi genocide so that future atrocities may be prevented.

Unfortunately, the historicity of the Holocaust has been undermined and chipped away at by the exact same sinister forces that created the genocide in the first place: racists, religious bigots and the most paranoid type of conspiracy theorists who, together, are uniting − often unwittingly − to form a new wave of anti-Semitism that will not willingly accept the obvious facts of the past.

This chipping away (at the truth) began slowly and insidiously – much like the Holocaust itself – but sadly, and worryingly, it is gathering pace.

A May, 2014 article in *The Atlantic*, headlined "The World Is Full of Holocaust Deniers," exposed some shocking statistics when it advised readers, "A new survey suggests that many Asians, Africans, Middle Easterners, young people, Muslims, and Hindus believe that facts about the genocide have been distorted."

The Atlantic columnist refers to a study conducted by First International Resources, which revealed that only "a third of the world's population believe the genocide has been accurately described in historical accounts. Some said they thought the number of people who died has been exaggerated; others said they believe it's a myth. Thirty percent of respondents said it's probably true that 'Jews still talk too much about what happened to them in the Holocaust'."

The article continues, "Seventy years after the liberation of Auschwitz, two-thirds of the world's population don't know the Holocaust happened—or they deny it. These beliefs follow some unexpected patterns, too. The Middle East and North Africa had the largest percentage of doubters, with only 8 percent of respondents reporting that they had heard of the genocide and believed descriptions of it were accurate. But only 12 percent of respondents in sub-Saharan Africa said the same, and only 23 percent in Asia. People in these groups were likely to say they believed the number of deaths has been exaggerated—just over half of Middle Easterners and a third of Asians and Africans think the body count has been distorted over time."

Another frightening statistic was mentioned by one Rainer Höss, grandson of Nazi war criminal and Auschwitz commandant Rudolf Höss, in a January 2016 article by Tal Bashan, of *the Jerusalem Post*, titled "Grandson of infamous Nazi spends lifetime making amends for namesake's atrocities."

Rainer, who is the antithesis of his grandfather and is devoting his life to promoting tolerance and Holocaust education, is quoted in the article as saying, "The current situation in Europe highlights the lessons of the Holocaust. In Germany alone, there are 360,000 active Nazis. In all of Europe, there are more than 2.6 million Nazis."

Bashan's article on Rainer Höss mentions that the Auschwitz commandant's grandson is constantly being contacted by anti-Semites who expect him to have the same hatred toward Jewish people that his grandfather had.

Rainer, who always wears the Star of David necklace he received from a Holocaust survivor, also says in *the Jerusalem Post* article that the family's former luxury villa near Auschwitz, where the death camp and crematoria could be viewed from during the war, is something "the management of the concentration camp doesn't like to publicize." He goes on to say that this is "because they're worried that neo-Nazis might turn this complex into a pilgrimage site."

As a society, we are in grave danger of fulfilling the pessimistic view of philosopher Friedrich Hegel who, as mentioned at the start of this book, wrote centuries ago that "The only thing we learn from history is that we learn nothing from history."

Holocaust deniers are sadly increasing, not decreasing around the world, and there is a war being waged against historical truth.

For example, Mark Weber, Director of the aforementioned leading Holocaust-denying organization the Institute for Historical Review, recently posted this boastful statement on the IHR's website: "In the weeks since our last update newsletter of mid-July [2015] ... I've conducted about twenty broadcast interviews, most of them with global television broadcasters that reach vast numbers of viewers ... In August I visited Istanbul, where I was the guest of a retired professor and former UNESCO official. During my week-long stay in the Turkish metropolis, I met with writers, scholars and human rights activists. One result was a lengthy interview with a journalist for a major Istanbul daily paper ... This four-part interview, with photos, appeared on two consecutive days' issues on the front page, and continuing on inside pages ... In the weeks since our last newsletter, we've organized three IHR meetings here in southern California."

The point being, Weber and his organization are expanding their reach and receiving plenty of airtime. There are, it seems, many around the world who are prepared to believe their message.

Within a decade or two, all Holocaust survivors will likely have passed away so a ticking clock is in effect in this battle between the truth and lies. Keep in mind even those survivors born in a concentration camp during WW2 would be at least 71 years-of-age when this book (the one you are reading now) was released. Those survivors old enough to clearly recall the events of that nightmare will, of course, be older and have much less time left.

As the memory of the Holocaust begins to fade away, it will become easier to deny the genocide even occurred *unless* those of us who are truthseekers are able to *embrace the memory* of the genocide and educate others do the same.

What's needed in this propaganda war is for the true stories of Holocaust survivors – as well as those of the Nazi perpetrators, their associates and others who witnessed the genocide – to be told loudly and clearly so that there will never, ever be room for doubt in generations to come. After all, nothing is more powerful, credible or damning than eyewitness accounts.

Eyewitness #1 must surely be US President Dwight D. Eisenhower who, during his time in Europe during WW2 served as Supreme Allied Commander and General of the United States Army, wrote the following letter, which we sourced on page 223 of Joseph P. Hobbs' book, *Dear General: Eisenhower's Wartime Letters to Marshall*:

"The visual evidence and the verbal testimony of starvation, cruelty and bestiality were so overpowering as to leave me a bit sick. In one room, where they [there] were piled up twenty or thirty naked men, killed by starvation, George Patton would not even enter. He said that he would get sick if he did so. I made the visit [to Gotha] deliberately, in order to be in a position to give first-hand evidence of these things if ever, in the future, there develops a tendency to charge these allegations merely to 'propaganda'."

It seems Eisenhower suspected there would be Holocaust deniers in the future and that propaganda would be their weapon of choice.

Above: *U.S. Generals including Eisenhower and Patton inspect charred corpses of Holocaust victims at Ohrdruf concentration camp.*

United States Holocaust Memorial Museum, courtesy of Harold Royall,

Licensed under Public Domain via Wikimedia Commons

If you, dear reader, are such a denier, or if you are considering there may be some truths in the deniers' theories, we say to you:

Stop falling for the propaganda of the anti-Semites – and believe us when we say those denialist groups and individuals identified and exposed throughout this book *are* anti-Semites. No getting around that.

Holocaust deniers will always come up with pathetic lies and red herrings aimed at deceiving and leading the gullible astray. Be it death toll anomalies, gas chamber debates, criticizing Holocaust denial laws, repeating the ancient myth that the "Joooz control the world," blaming Israel, claiming Anne Frank's diary is fabricated etc...etc...yada...yada...yawn...the list goes on.

There's literally no end to the lies and red herrings the deniers throw up. As each lie or distortion of the truth is debunked, these people keep searching for more and more. We have seen this many, many times – literally hundreds of times in recent history – as more and more denial arguments are raised only to be shot down.

Why do the deniers persist? Because they have an agenda – and it isn't a nice agenda, we can assure you.

As previously stated, if the Jews were not the main victims of the Holocaust, nobody would be debating this. The Jewish people are easily one of the most hated ethnic/religious groups in the world. As outlined in chapter 7, throughout the centuries before the Holocaust the Jews endured two millennia of persecution during which many other genocides, or ethnic cleansings, were committed against them.

So, if you are a denier, *get on the right side of history* and stop being so gullible.

Remember, it has been historically and scientifically proven, in a court of law no less, that more than 1.2 million Jews, along with 20,000 gypsies and tens of thousands of Polish and Russian political prisoners, were killed at Auschwitz alone. Beyond that, Yad Vashem's *Central Database of Shoah Victims' Names* has collected 4.5 million Jewish victims' names (and counting) from various archival sources.

How much more evidence could you possibly want?

Six million Jews died in the Holocaust. Yet many people simply cannot accept this. They keep bringing up red herring after red herring to avoid finally admitting "YES, it happened exactly as the history books say, end of story." Which, of course, is the only correct response to the question anti-Semites raise about whether or not this *historically and forensically-proven* Nazi genocide even happened.

"However intrinsically loony an idea may be, when people believe it, and act on that belief, it attains a power that can shape reality around it. A simple case in point is Nazi anti-Semitism. The fringe and utterly bogus notion that Jews represented a kind of biological contamination that had to be eradicated root and branch became the operative philosophy of a political regime and as a result millions of people died."

–Richard B. Spence, The Orphan Conspiracies: 29 Conspiracy Theories from The Orphan Trilogy

We would like to give the final word in this book to a friend of ours, one Pam Blevins, who is a Museum Teacher Fellow for the United States Holocaust Memorial Museum, and who posted the following insightful summary on the book-readers social media site *Goodreads*:

"The Holocaust did happen and the gas chambers were in use. There are eyewitnesses to this fact although they are rapidly dying. The reason the Holocaust is so important is that it specifically refers to the approximately 6 million Jews who were killed. Many were gassed or shot, many others died of overwork, malnutrition, diseases, etc. It is a fact that the Nazis wanted to exterminate the entire Jewish 'race'. WWII resulted in an additional 5 million others killed by the same processes. This does not count the military losses on all sides. If you doubt, take a trip to Germany and Poland and see the labor camps and death camps. See the gas chambers still in existence. During the trial of Deborah Lipstadt vs David Irving in England in 2000, Deborah Lipstadt had to prove her statement that David Irving was a Holocaust denier. He was proved to be wrong in his assertions that the Holocaust did not exist. Visit any of the Holocaust museums around the country and in Jerusalem for the facts. Check with the countries, especially Germany, where denying the Holocaust is a crime. I am not Jewish; but I have studied WWII and the Holocaust extensively. I am a museum teacher and was a Regional Educator for the United States Holocaust Memorial Museum. I have studied in Germany and Israel, I have visited many of the camps and ghettos in Germany and Poland. I have read over 500 books by various authors on the Holocaust. I have heard personal testimony from a variety of survivors. I have heard many acclaimed historians speak. The Holocaust did occur and was planned and executed by the Nazi regime. It did include shootings, torture, starvation, working people to death, and gas chambers."

Peace,

James Morcan & Lance Morcan

THE END

OTHER BOOKS

BY JAMES & LANCE MORCAN PUBLISHED BY STERLING GATE BOOKS

Non-fiction:

The Orphan Conspiracies: 29 Conspiracy Theories from The Orphan Trilogy

GENIUS INTELLIGENCE: Secret Techniques and Technologies to Increase IQ (The Underground Knowledge Series, #1)

ANTIGRAVITY PROPULSION: Human or Alien Technologies? (The Underground Knowledge Series, #2)

MEDICAL INDUSTRIAL COMPLEX: The $ickness Industry, Big Pharma and Suppressed Cures (The Underground Knowledge Series, #3)

The Catcher in the Rye Enigma: J.D. Salinger's Mind Control Triggering Device or a Coincidental Literary Obsession of Criminals? (The Underground Knowledge Series, #4)

INTERNATIONAL BANKSTER$: The Global Banking Elite Exposed and the Case for Restructuring Capitalism (The Underground Knowledge Series, #5)

BANKRUPTING THE THIRD WORLD: How the Global Elite Drown Poor Nations in a Sea of Debt (The Underground Knowledge Series, #6)

UNDERGROUND BASES: Subterranean Military Facilities and the Cities Beneath Our Feet (The Underground Knowledge Series, #7)

Historical fiction:

Into the Americas (A novel based on a true story)

World Odyssey (The World Duology, #1)

Fiji: A Novel (The World Duology, #2)

White Spirit (A novel based on a true story)

Thrillers:

The Ninth Orphan (The Orphan Trilogy, #1)

The Orphan Factory (The Orphan Trilogy, #2)

The Orphan Uprising (The Orphan Trilogy, #3)